The Ultimate Guide to

Rally-O

Rules, Strategies, and Skills for Successful Rally Obedience Competition

Debra M. Eldredge, DVM

The Ultimate Guide to Rally-O

Project Team
Editor: Stephanie Fornino
Copy Editor: Joann Woy
Indexer: Elizabeth Walker
Designer: Mary Ann Kahn

T.F.H. Publications
President/CEO: Glen S. Axelrod
Executive Vice President: Mark E. Johnson
Publisher: Christopher T. Reggio
Production Manager: Kathy Bontz

TFH Publications, Inc.
One TFH Plaza
Third and Union Avenues
Neptune City, NJ 07753

Printed and bound in China
11 12 13 14 15 16 1 3 5 7 9 8 6 4 2

Library of Congress Cataloging-in-Publication Data
Eldredge, Debra.
The ultimate guide to rally-o: rules, strategies, and skills for successful rally obedience competition / Deb M. Eldredge.
p. cm.
Includes index.
ISBN 978-0-7938-0648-5 (alk. paper)
1. Rally (Dog sport) 2. Dogs--Training. I. Title.
SF425.85.R35E53 2011
791.8--dc22
2010026954

This book has been published with the intent to provide accurate and authoritative information in regard to the subject matter within. While every reasonable precaution has been taken in preparation of this book, the author and publisher expressly disclaim responsibility for any errors, omissions, or adverse effects arising from the use or application of the information contained herein. The techniques and suggestions are used at the reader's discretion and are not to be considered a substitute for veterinary care. If you suspect a medical problem consult your veterinarian.

Note: In the interest of concise writing, "he" is used when referring to puppies and dogs unless the text is specifically referring to females or males. "She" is used when referring to people. However, the information contained herein is equally applicable to both sexes.

The Leader In Responsible Animal Care For Over 50 Years!®
wwww.tfh.com
CENTRAL Garden & Pet

Table of Contents

16
Sit
15
Off-Set
Figure 8

Laying the Foundation

What Is Rally?

What exactly is rally, the exciting new dog sport sweeping the country? The American Kennel Club (AKC) has this to say: "Rally is a sport in which the dog and handler complete a course that has been designed by the rally judge." The Canadian Association of Rally Obedience (CARO) goes a step further with: "Rally obedience is a fun dog obedience sport, open to ALL dogs, purebred or mixed breed, pets or titled champions as well as physically challenged dogs and/or handlers." From the Association of Pet Dog Trainers (APDT) we get: "APDT rally is a fun and exciting team sport for dogs and their handlers!"

But I feel that rally is best described by first looking at one of the Webster dictionary's definitions of rally: "To join in a common cause." I personally define rally as a fun dog sport in which a dog and handler team negotiate a course of obedience-type exercises, with the handler free to inspire, encourage, and praise the canine half of the team.

The concept of rally as a dog sport is that it emphasizes the positive interaction and close bond between handler and dog while performing a set of exercises designated on simple signs (known as *stations*) set along a numbered course. Many of the exercises are challenging for the handler to remember and for the dog to execute—at least at the higher levels. A little bit of obedience, a little bit of agility, and LOTS of fun!

The beginning level of rally in all organizations can be done on lead, making it a wonderful beginner sport for dogs and their people. The exercises that are designated on the signs for each station include obedience moves, agility moves, and fun moves. Much of what you see on a rally course used to be called "doodling" by obedience trainers who wanted to work on precision and specific moves with their dogs without doing boring and repetitive drills. They were looking for ways to improve precision but not dampen their dogs' enthusiasm. Rally provides a fun way to help you and your dog achieve the teamwork that can lead to greater successes in obedience and agility competitions, as well as in rally competition itself.

So rally is a sport in which a dog-and-handler team follows a set course designated by signs that describe exercises to perform and that guide the team's movement. Numbers are used to guide the team in the correct flow from station to station. For many people, rally is a sport unto itself, not merely a stepping stone to higher obedience or a way to strengthen training for agility. I have participated in rally with a young puppy, a dog in the middle of her active career, and also with an older, retired dog. I found it to be fun and rewarding for all of my dogs. That, I believe, is the real appeal of rally—it can be fun for literally *every* dog and handler, and all dogs are capable of participating.

The History of Rally

How did rally get its start? We can credit Charles (Bud) Kramer. Back in 1999, Bud Kramer came up with an idea to take some obedience moves and create a sport that was fun for dog and handler. Starting from a car rally perspective, Mr. Kramer felt that obedience needed a fun way to "jump-start" competitors. He envisioned active communication between dog and handler throughout this course and judges with the freedom to create unique and flowing courses. Scoring was to avoid the precision hassles that turn many people off to competitive obedience. Levels were to be set up for a gradual progression in training and successes along the way. Bud Kramer was also the first person to introduce agility to the United States, so the idea of fun dog sports, courses with flow, minimal judge interaction, and plenty of dog–handler communication was not new to him.

The February 2000 issue of *Front and Finish* magazine introduced rally to the dog world at large. Mr. Kramer published a novel idea: an obedience-type course with directional signs that a dog and handler would run without direct judge input, one that allowed plenty of encouragement for the dog—a more natural form of obedience, if you will. After all, most of us talk to and encourage our dogs in training and in real-life situations when we need some obedience. The course design helped handlers to work on specific areas without doing multiple repetitions of the exact same movement.

The APDT picked up the ball almost immediately, starting with trials toward titling in 2001. The CARO was up and running in 2002. The World Wide Kennel Club (WWKC) started offering trials in 2003. The AKC followed in 2005. The Canadian Kennel Club (CKC) held its first rally trials in 2007. Although the CKC is limited to approved purebred dogs, the AKC, APDT, CARO, United Kennel Club (UKC), and Australian Shepherd Club of America (ASCA) all allow mixed-breed dogs who are spayed or neutered to participate in their activities. In the case of the ASCA, that even includes dogs who are not Australian Shepherds or Australian Shepherd mixes.

Rally Speak

You may see rally referred to as "rally," "rally-o," or "rally obedience." All of these terms refer to the same fun dog sport.

Basic Rules of the Sport

Rally truly does appeal to a wide range of dog handlers. The beginning levels of the sport in all organizations start out with the dogs on lead. By allowing verbal encouragement, patting your leg, and in some cases even offering food rewards between stations, this is a very user-friendly entry into the world of dog sports for both novice handlers and their canine partners. It is also an ideal starting point for more experienced handlers who wish to eventually move on to competitive sports such as obedience or agility. Some organizations also make accommodations for handlers or dogs with disabilities. Scoring is generally kept loose enough to prevent discouragement, but individual handlers may choose to hold their dogs to a tighter standard.

As you move up the levels, the exercises to be performed are more complex, and dogs may have to work off lead. Low jumps are added, and dogs may have to work a short distance away from their handlers. Still, encouraging and talking to your dog is allowed, and attitude is considered very important. A dog competing in rally should always look interested, focused on his handler and the job at hand, and happy to be out working!

Your Goal as Handler

Your basic goal as a handler is to follow the course correctly, taking all of the numbered signs in order and ideally performing all of the exercises as required. Along the way, you must strive to keep your dog's focus on you and his attitude up. While course runs are timed, organizations have generous or no time limits. Time may be used to break a tie, but a higher score will always place higher than a run that is faster but has a lower score. In the CARO and APDT, adjustments in the course, including extra time allowed, can be made for a handler or dog with a disability. If you get lost on course, you can quickly look at the number of the last sign you did, then scan around for the next number. Ideally, you get a feel for the flow of the course while walking it, but it is not uncommon for people to get lost when they first start rally. A well-designed course will flow along very naturally, but some courses can be quite challenging.

Rally Signs

In rally, most of the signs will be placed on your right-hand side so that you, not your dog, are next to the sign. This lessens the chance of your dog knocking a sign over and also gives you a clear chance to read the sign as you approach. There are a few exceptions. Change-of-direction signs, such as turns, are usually placed directly in your path so that you can't miss them—perhaps also as a hint that they are changes of direction! Exercises should be performed near the signs—this is generally taken to mean within 2 to 4 feet (.5 to 1 m) of the sign. A few signs will be performed farther away—the 1,2,3 Steps Backward and the Call Front, Back Up will end up away from the sign.

Cone exercises, such as the Spiral, Weaves, and Off-Set Figure 8, may require you to enter with the sign on your left. On any Weave exercise, the first cone should be on your left, and often it is convenient to simply put the sign by the cone. For the Spiral, the sign is usually to your left as well.

Common Moves

The common moves your dog will need to know include *sit*, *lie down*, *stand,* and *stay*, as well as walking with you under control. While walking with you, your dog will have to do changes of pace—moving slowly or quickly as the signs require. You and your dog will also have to master turns. These range from simple 90-degree left and right turns to complicated spins such as 180-, 270-, and 360-degree turns. Most dogs catch on quickly and find turns to be fun, especially those that make humans dizzy!

Titles

At the first level, the AKC offers an RN title for the Rally Novice level. In the

Rally Caution

Rally should be fun! If you find yourself frustrated or not smiling, take a break and simply play a game with your dog.

APDT, the first title is an R-1 for Rally Level 1. In the CARO, the RN is used again for a Rally Novice title. In both the CARO and the APDT, you may see CL or MCL added onto the title. The CL stands for "cum laude" or "with honor," and the MCL stands for "magna cum laude" or "with highest honor." Those additions are based on the scores your dog has achieved while earning his title.

A Level Playing Field

One of the biggest bonuses about rally is that the playing field is fairly level for all breeds of dogs and for all handlers. Handlers may vary from card-carrying members of the AARP to young juniors just starting out. I have seen dogs from very large Irish Wolfhounds to very small Chihuahuas competing in rally, all with equal chances for placements and titles. Most organizations allow mixed breeds, and some of the organizations, as mentioned previously, even make allowances for dogs with disabilities. Many top obedience and agility breeds, such as Border Collies, Shetland Sheepdogs, and Papillons, excel at rally, but top dogs in rally include Rottweilers, Bernese Mountain Dogs, Bulldogs, and many mixed breeds.

As I mentioned, at my first AKC Rally® trials, I ran three dogs: my 7-month-old Belgian Tervuren puppy, my 6-year-old Belgian Tervuren, and my 13-year-old Pembroke Welsh Corgi. The whole gamut—from puppy starting out to retired older dog! All three dogs enjoyed working in rally, and it showed just how appealing the sport is to dogs of all ages. For a young dog, it is an excellent way to start competing in strange places and having to concentrate on his work while still having the backup of plenty of verbal support and encouragement. For dogs who are in between competitive obedience levels or who simply need to restore some confidence, rally is perfect. And for the retired dog, rally is a very nonstressful way to get out, compete, and be part of the whole dog competition scene that many of them love and have missed.

How to Get Started

If rally sounds like a sport you and your dog might enjoy, you have a number of ways to get started. To train or compete in rally, get a set of signs showing the specific exercises you need to complete. You will eventually want to print out a set of signs to set up, but you can start by simply training the exercises from descriptions such as are provided later in this book. The signs are set up as a course you must follow, displayed in numbered sign holders. While following a rally course, the judge will not give you additional directions beyond "Are you ready?" and "Forward." You pace yourself, ideally moving briskly about the course, doing the exercises in the correct order while praising and encouraging your dog. At the lower levels, you are allowed to pat your leg, clap, and chirp and chatter as much as you need to keep your dog working with you on a loose lead. In the APDT, you are even allowed to give a small food reward after some stations. As you move up in levels, the exercises become more advanced and the amount of overt help and encouragement you can provide to your dog is limited, but verbal encouragement and assistance are always allowed.

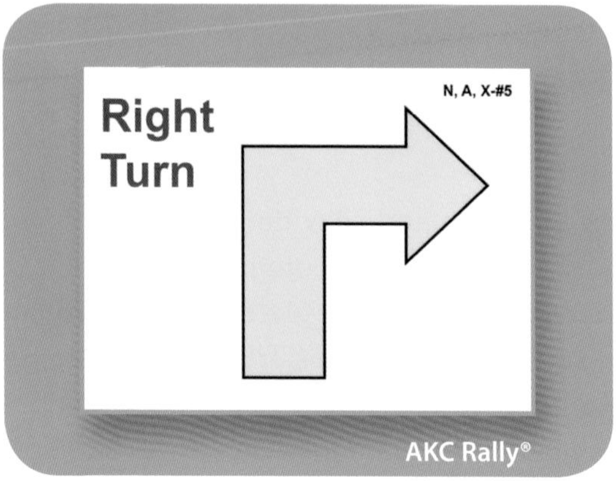

Signs

Most of the signs have visual as well as written directives to guide you. At first, rally may feel like the old kid's challenge of walking, talking, and chewing gum at the same time, but it quickly becomes a fun time with your dog. While the performance of each exercise is judged, the judging is not as precise or tough as it is for obedience. Attitude, clear enjoyment of the sport, and teamwork are emphasized, even earning bonus points in some venues. Every course is unique, using different combinations of the approved exercises. Judges have a list of exercises to choose from and can arrange the course as they wish. An ideal rally course is challenging but also has a smooth flow to it. You and your dog should never be bored with the wide variety of courses possible!

How to Find a Class

This book will help you with the basics and give you chances to see just how versatile the rally format can be. Check with your local dog clubs or dog training facilities to see if they offer rally classes. Check out the rally organization websites to see if any competitions are coming up in your area. Attending a competition to watch can inspire you to train and compete yourself and will give you a way to meet local people with similar interests.

Finding a rally class is easy in most areas. Check telephone book listings or search online for local dog training clubs. With the rising popularity of rally, most clubs offer classes to the public. Expect to pay for classes, although fees vary greatly. For kids, many 4-H clubs offer dog training, including rally. Some kennels and some kennel clubs will have rally classes as well. Private trainers may offer rally classes, in addition to obedience and agility.

If no local classes or resources are available, find a training buddy, print out or order a set of signs (see Resources), and off you go! Realistically, all you need are your dog, a collar, a leash, this book, a few signs and holders (although you can start learning the moves without the signs, it is easier to glance at them periodically), and some treats or toys to keep your dog enthused.

Supplies You'll Need

Before you head off to class, make sure that you have the required equipment. Your instructor may advise you about specific things, but some items are basic to training in general.

Collar

Most rally classes suggest a buckle collar or mild training collar such as a nylon slip collar. (Slip collars aren't recommended outside rally—and *never* use one unless you have been trained to do so by a professional trainer.) APDT

These are examples of acceptable collars.

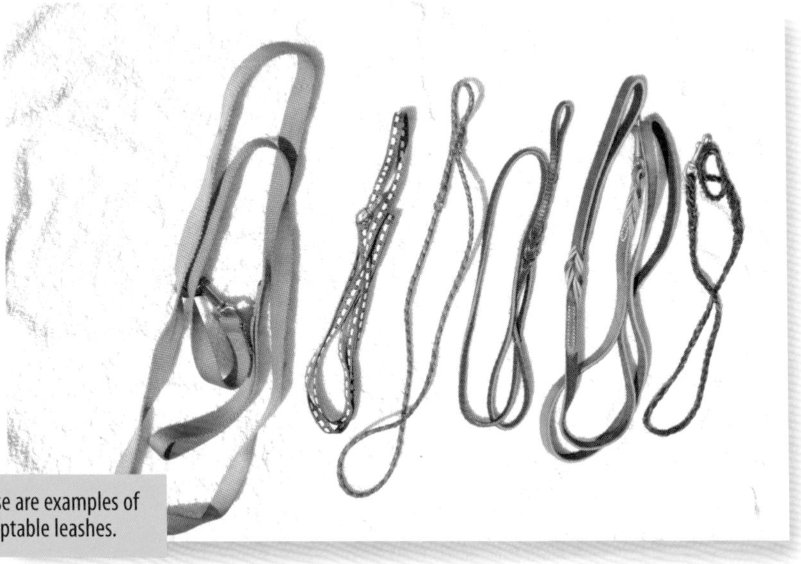

These are examples of acceptable leashes.

trials will require a plain flat collar with a buckle or quick release. The AKC will allow training collars such as a chain or nylon slip collar. You can train with any collar you and your dog are comfortable with, but know the requirements of any venues in which you might compete.

Leash

Have a comfortable leash—comfortable for *your* hands! Leather, braided, or plain is generally comfortable, and many nylon leashes are easy on the hands, too. A plastic handle or a chain leash is not. Retractable leashes may be used for training some exercises but should not be used for travel or most training. Some exercises will require a 6-foot (2-m) lead, but I find a shorter lead is easier for most training. That way neither you nor your dog will get tangled! Choose a leash of reasonable weight for your dog. Your Chihuahua will do well on a thin nylon lead as opposed to a 2-inch-wide (5-cm) leather lead. On the other hand, don't count on that thin lead holding your young male Rottweiler! Look at the snap size on the lead as well. A large snap can be distracting and heavy for a toy dog.

Food

Ask the instructor ahead of time about the use of food and toys in class. Most instructors want you to have something to positively motivate your dog. Don't forget that you should always have with you praise and your hands for petting too! Choose treats that are small —you don't want an overweight rally dog! Ideally, a treat can be quickly swallowed and is something your dog really likes. It can help to keep certain special treats just for training times. For toys, choose one that encourages the dog to interact with you. A soft tug toy works well for many dogs, and you can make one yourself braiding fleece scraps. Make sure that your dog knows to stop tugging when you call the end of the game.

Although many dogs are thrilled about balls of any size and color, throwing a ball around in a room full of dogs may not be the best idea. Remember that *all* of the dogs may want the ball, and you don't want to cause a major distraction. The same goes for most squeaky toys.

Water and Bowl

It is a good idea to bring some water from home and a bowl so that your dog can have a drink. Training is hard work for your dog! Our dogs enjoy a 1-gallon (4-l) thermos filled with ice water. With a wide-mouthed one, most dogs can simply drink from the jug.

Rally Profile

Dalena and Her Italian Greyhounds

At the very first rally trials held by the American Kennel Club (AKC)—at midnight on January 1, 2005, in Rochester, New York, Dalena had the honor—or the scare!—of being the first person to run an AKC Rally® course. Her Italian Greyhound Davis was equal to the task and qualified. For the record, he was followed by an Irish Wolfhound. Dalena has continued on in rally, putting Rally Excellent titles on two of her Italian Greyhounds.

Dalena chose to try rally because it looked like a fun activity to do with her dogs and a true team sport. She enjoys the fact that she can talk to her dogs while training and trailing. Many of the exercises are fun and challenging. "For my dogs, the stationary exercises, especially when they have to sit or even sit more than once, are hard to train and not so much fun. Getting a true *down* with the elbows down can be tricky also. Italian Greyhounds like to move!" And don't even mention wet or cold weather—to these little dogs with no warm coat or insulation of fat, those are not acceptable working conditions.

Luckily, Dalena's Italian Greyhounds do like food, and using treats in training helps them to be successful. Dalena also tries to find behaviors that the dogs offer independently and then reinforces them with jackpots.

Training and competing in rally has made Dalena and her dogs tighter as a team. "This increase in teamwork has helped us in agility too," reports Dalena. "Rally gave me the confidence to start obedience training with my dogs and really helped me learn to work with them."

Trials, as long as the conditions suit her canine partners, are lots of fun, although some can go on for a long day. Dalena's dogs are now working on the RAE titles so that they get to do both Advanced B and Excellent B rally. Her dogs especially love getting to jump because they can almost fly! Serpentines are another fun sign because they can zip right along. The Side Step Right has been tricky for both Dalena and the dogs to learn and is their least favorite sign.

Dalena offers some comments and suggestions for others with small or toy dogs, especially ones without a lot of coat. These dogs are affected by cold, wet, or even damp conditions because they can chill easily. Even a cold floor indoors is uncomfortable for them. While you can't always avoid those conditions at trials, certainly avoid them in training so that your dog doesn't make negative associations between training and physical discomfort. "When working on the *down*, you need to be sure that the elbows are actually touching the floor or ground each and every time!" That is true for all dogs, although the dogs with lots of coat may sneak by once in a while.

For those who are doing rally with Italian Greyhounds specifically, Dalena has additional words of wisdom. "Italian Greyhounds really do love to move, so courses that flow right along are more fun for them and for me. Don't forget that while tiny, they are sighthounds. They notice things outside of the ring and can be easily distracted. Italian Greyhounds are also independent thinkers and problem solvers. This makes them fun but a challenge to train!"

Crate

A crate is important. Your dog will need to be put somewhere while you walk the course, learn the signs yourself, and listen to the instructor. Ideally, you already have a lightweight crate that collapses so that it is easy for you to carry in and set up. Some dogs can be trusted in a tent or canvas crate, but don't try those unless your dog is calm and steady in a crate. We have found that the collapsible Nylabone crates work well for our dogs when they are young and not so trustworthy. Wire crates are cool for hot weather, while plastic kennels provide protection from cold weather and wind.

Doggy Seat Belt

Your dog should travel to class in a crate or with a doggy seat belt while in the car. A loose dog is a danger to himself and to you if there is a crash.

Prepare for Your Class

If at all possible, watch a class or two *before* you sign up. Look for an instructor who is clear but who makes the class fun. Be sure that you are comfortable with whatever training techniques are used. Also, look for safety and comfort. Are the dogs in class under control but happy? Is the footing safe for people and dogs? A cold barn with deep sawdust may not be the ideal training location for you and your Italian Greyhound.

The instructor should be knowledgeable and experienced in rally. Hopefully, handouts will be distributed so that you can practice at home during the week. If an instructor, the methods, or anything about the class makes you feel uncomfortable, keep on looking.

It is also a good idea to contact the various rally organizations and order their rulebooks. These are generally quite inexpensive and include guidelines to competing and explanations of their signs and exercises. Some include training tips as well. You will need a copy of the rulebook to study before you enter any competitions.

The websites of the organizations may include rulebooks that you can download for free and print out for your personal use. These sites may also have signs that you can download and print on your own. Printing on sturdy card stock and then laminating the signs will give you an inexpensive set with which to practice and train.

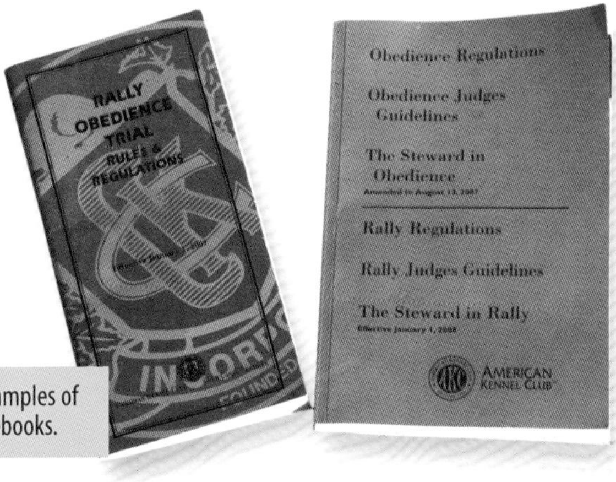

These are examples of common rulebooks.

80

Why Try Rally?

2

Let's face it—the modern household has plenty of ways to fill up spare time. So why try rally with your dog? There are many reasons. A well-trained rally dog has skills that are useful around the house and out in public. The rally dog can function despite distractions and is steady around other dogs and people (even if he isn't a real extrovert, he knows how to behave and control himself). With the increased emphasis on fitness, a rally trainer and dog can both get a bit of a workout while having fun together.

Beyond the exact training and new skills a rally dog learns, an incredible bond of love and understanding is built when you and your dog work through a challenge. Communicating with another species to accomplish a common goal is extremely rewarding, and some of the techniques might work with your human teenager too! Dogs have been selected over many generations to work with and for their human partners, and they thrive on work and companionship.

Rally is also a sport that fits the physical abilities of most people and most dogs. You don't have to be a marathon runner or top sprinter like some of the top agility competitors, and your dog may simply be a semi-couch dog. The physical demands are kept reasonable so that dogs of all shapes and sizes can compete. Some venues even make accommodations for dogs with disabilities and give extra time or other adjustments for handlers who might have a disability. Rally is intended to be all-inclusive, with awards achievable by all teams but with special incentives for teams that choose to strive for excellence in this sport. Both senior handlers and junior handlers can enjoy rally with their dogs.

Rally is fun for senior handlers and their dogs.

Younger Dogs

For a young dog having to face the stress of competition along with travel, new dogs, new places, etc., rally is the perfect introductory sport. You can encourage, inspire, and support your dog verbally in the ring in all venues. In some venues, such as the APDT, you can even give a food treat at certain points on the course. Rally is not physically demanding, so while you are waiting for bone growth plates to close, your dog can still be learning all about teamwork and different body movements.

Rally Speak

"Verbal" can mean distinct words, chirps, clicks, and silly sounds.

Dogs grow, literally, from the ends of their bones. At the ends of the long bones such as the femur and humerus there are areas called "growth plates." In this area are cells that divide and add to the length of the bone. When the dog has reached his final size, these areas will close. During the growth phase, these areas are very sensitive to trauma. If the cells get damaged, growth might stop. This could leave a dog with one leg shorter than the others. For this reason, you don't want to encourage a lot of jumping in a young dog.

Doing Spirals and Weaves rally style helps teach a young giant-breed dog, such as a Great Dane, exactly where his feet are and how to coordinate his movements without stressing his growing body. Remember to be patient with the large- and giant-breed dogs because these puppies often have to "grow into" coordination. A toy breed can develop confidence to move in the world of bigger dogs by observing other dogs from ringside and then competing safely himself. A sense of accomplishment, accompanied by your praise, is good for the self-esteem of every dog.

Breed rescue dogs and shelter adoptees may face some of the same confidence issues that many young dogs do. Again, rally is an ideal way for them to gain confidence and learn to deal with people, dogs, and activity in a safe situation. You are right with them, a supportive partner, at all times.

Older Dogs

Rally is an ideal sport for older dogs. The physical demands are minimal. Even at the higher levels, the jumps are quite low. If even the rally jumping is too much, most organizations will allow you to stay at the novice level and continue to work toward championships and other titles and awards. A dog with vision problems will still be receiving many verbal assists, and a deaf dog can get plenty of hand signals and visual guides. In both the CARO and APDT, adjustments can be made to help accommodate a handler or dog with a disability, including extra time allowed. In all venues, courses can be arranged to allow a wheelchair to run the course. Just make sure that the judge knows ahead of time so that she can adjust her course as needed.

Many older dogs may need the extra encouragement allowed in rally to get themselves psyched up to work and compete. Others are simply thrilled that they are the "dog of the day" and are getting to attend training classes and competitions again. With time primarily used to break ties, the older dog who works steadily and accurately is not penalized and may even come through to win awards. A dog approaching double digits may not be able to run an Excellent agility course, but he may find rally just as much fun because he can still travel with you on weekends and get to enjoy competing with you. It is also good for older dogs to keep active, both for their mental status and to keep those older joints moving and supple. Arthritic joints tend to do better with moderate, regular exercise, and rally can certainly fill the bill.

Giant-breed dogs, such as this Bernese Mountain Dog, can learn to coordinate their movements by doing rally.

When training in rally with an older dog, consider carefully his age and capabilities. My older Corgi felt that she had about six *sits* per day to do in training or competitions. So I had to carefully plan my training so as not to stress or demotivate her. Our warm-ups at trials never included *sits* because I didn't want to "waste" any. It was tricky running some of the courses with plenty of *sits* included! I learned to be very creative in my encouragement.

Along with older dogs, dogs who have had injuries or simply show the wear and tear of years of competition may find rally physically within their capabilities and more in their comfort level. These dogs may no longer be able to clear the jump heights required in agility or obedience but can do the rally exercises without any problem. This way, they are still mentally challenged by training and competing, and emotionally secure as they get to train and compete with you. Dogs want to be with us and to work together—rally is the ideal way to do that. Always check with your veterinarian to be sure that an older or injured dog can do the rally exercises without any physical harm.

Control and Fun

In virtually all dog sports, a dog must learn to focus and concentrate on his work and usually his human partner. In rally, the human partner can freely help her dog remember to pay attention and do his part by giving plenty of positive verbal encouragement. Although rally runs tend to move along briskly, there is still plenty of time to help your dog focus and do the exercises.

Whether your favorite dog sport is fieldwork, agility, herding, or any of the other great dog activities, your dog must learn control. In rally, the novice dog is automatically somewhat controlled by the leash, but in addition, you can use your voice and hands to help keep him with you and working on the task at hand. Your goal is control and enthusiasm on a loose leash. Many of the rally exercises, especially as you move up in levels, require a fair amount of control by the dog—both in his attention and in his body movements. He learns to make fairly precise turns and twists while paying attention to where his partner is and how you are moving.

Through rally, your dog learns physical control of his body to make some of the movements required and learns mental control so that he stays with you on course. And you have the option at all times of verbally helping and encouraging him! The speed of a rally course is slow enough that you can guide (and lure in some venues) if need be and help your dog figure out where to put his feet and how to perform so that he stays with you as a team. While

Rally Profile

Jenna and Keeper

Jenna was just nine years old when she started in rally. Her family has a lovely male Belgian Tervuren named Sensation's Keeper of My Heart CD RN, or Keeper for short. Keeper is a true family dog, doing obedience with Jenna's Mom, agility with Jenna's sister Alexa, and rally with Jenna. Jenna wanted to be involved with Keeper, and rally seemed to be the perfect dog sport for her. It is fun, but relatively easy to get started in. You can train almost anywhere, and it was a sport that Keeper hadn't tried yet.

Jenna says, "I like rally because it is relaxed and not stressful—at least most of the time! It is fun." Still, there are challenges in doing rally with a dog like a Belgian Tervuren, who has plenty of energy and work drive. "For me, it can be a challenge to keep my dog's interest. Now that Keeper and I have earned our RN and will be out of Novice, the course will be more interesting to him."

For Jenna and Keeper, rally is a good sport because Keeper loves to work. If she makes it fun, he enjoys doing it. On the other hand, if Jenna is not upbeat in her training or acts bored, Keeper quickly gets bored too.

Keeper knew many of the novice exercises from the obedience training Jenna's Mom had done with him. He had to learn to work with Jenna, though, and Jenna had to work hard on her handling. Jenna has now had plenty of practice in making sure that Keeper concentrates on her and what they are doing in the ring despite distractions. Training in rally has also helped Jenna gain dog sense and be aware of her dog and what he might be thinking at all times. Belgian Tervurens are very alert dogs and notice just about everything in their environment. Keeping them focused on you is a challenge. Luckily, rally keeps you moving and provides plenty for your dog to think about and do.

This year, Jenna and Keeper earned the RN or Rally Novice title in AKC competition. They even had placements competing against adults! Jenna feels that rally competitions are very exciting. She recommends that you study your course, know the flow pattern, read the signs carefully, and really "talk it up with your dog." Verbal encouragement and praise are extremely important, especially if you are both nervous!

training, you may find that you need to go quite slowly or even break exercises and movements down into parts so that your dog has time to figure out his part of the job. As you both gain confidence and experience, you can work at moving faster.

Rally as Foundation Sport

Although rally is a fun sport on its own, it has incredible value as a foundation for many other dog activities. In obedience, agility, and freestyle, dogs must work with their human partners but also be able to work away at times while still maintaining attention on their handlers. Rally incorporates those elements right from the start with various finishes, unique turns, and unusual movements. In a controlled atmosphere and at a reasonable speed, your dog learns to focus on you while still being able to perform a physical exercise.

Many of the rally exercises were developed from what was called "doodling" in obedience—silly turns, spins, and movements that help a dog learn to maintain *heel* position, keep attention on the handler, and build body awareness. The goal for obedience is to build precision but without boring, repetitive exercises. Rally takes those exercises and turns them into a fun competition. Because rally requires movements and turns in both directions, your dog will be better balanced physically than a dog who simply works in obedience.

This body awareness and ability to work while still maintaining contact with the handler are essential for a top agility dog. Spins, unique turns, and smooth transitions are also important for a top freestyle performance. Freestyle is another dog sport in which a dog must work equally well on both sides of his handler.

Rally can also simply be for fun, with no aim toward competition. Imagine a rally course with signs like "Dog Sit, Handler Sing Happy Birthday" or "Dog Down, Handler Put on Hat" with a funny hat on the chair at the station. Once you have the rally concept in mind, there is no end to the fun ways you can work with your dog. A silly rally course can be a great way to end a training session, dog camp day, or 4-H training demo. Let your imagination run wild.

Advantages of Rally Work

The advantages of using rally as your basic foundation training are many. Your dog will tend to have a positive attitude and look forward to training sessions and competitions. He will learn to work despite some stress because you can still provide verbal encouragement even at competitions when you are nervous yourself. Your dog will be aware of his body and be able to do some physical movements that will keep him supple and will help him work on coordination. You, as a handler, will learn to be aware of many things at once—basically you will become a master of multitasking as you read signs, move along, encourage your dog, and do the exercises. If you tend to be a "visual person," the signs will usually show what your task is. If you are better at reading quickly, the short written descriptions should be adequate.

If you like competing with your dog, the rally ringside atmosphere tends to be a bit less competitive than those of the obedience or agility rings. Many competitors are using rally primarily to help train a young dog, to build confidence and self-esteem in a shy dog, or to keep their veteran out competing and happy. While earning titles is certainly a goal for most exhibitors, top honors are generally not as important as in some other dog sports. There will be some people

A rally foundation can help your dog in obedience later.

for whom excelling in rally competition is a goal. Watch these teams because these will be exhibitors striving for precision in their performance but also using various techniques to keep their dogs enthusiastic. Most of these top-notch competitors are very willing to share training tips with a novice, but wait until after their runs.

Rally is an excellent starting point for training toward many types of dog competitions. It can be done as a sport in itself or lead you to greater success in obedience, agility, and freestyle. The progression of levels in most organizations is rational and even so that your dog gradually takes on more responsibility for your performance. If you choose to work on precision, you can—and that may help you in competitive obedience.

Disadvantages of Rally Work

There are some disadvantages to rally work, but they are few and minor. Some dogs become dependent on your verbal assistance and need to be weaned off gradually and carefully so that they maintain their attitude and confidence. Dogs who have worked in rally are used to very short heeling sequences with lots of unusual moves to keep them alert and tuned into you. For competitive obedience, they must learn to maintain focus without lots of new input—either verbally or from motion. For agility, your dog needs to add in working away from you at a greater distance unless you are *very* athletic yourself and can run with him.

One disadvantage I had not thought of until I started showing my young dog in obedience is that rally dogs are not used to the judge giving commands other than the initial "Forward." Hokey looked at the judge very strangely

Rally Caution

Dogs who have only worked in rally may be a bit put off by the judge giving commands throughout your run in obedience. Practice with a pretend judge to cover for this.

when she kept telling us to "Go forward" or "Halt!" That was quickly remedied, however.

You will have to remind yourself not to give lots of verbal encouragement while you are competing in obedience. In obedience, you are allowed to praise and encourage your dog between exercises but not during them as you can in rally. For a dog who needs plenty of positive feedback, try entering both a rally class and an obedience class at a trial. That way, he will get lots of reinforcement during at least one performance in the ring. You can also use your rally run to focus on areas that were difficult in the obedience competition. A little extra encouragement might help with those right turns or changes of pace.

The time required to set up a rally course at home can be a small disadvantage. And if it is a windy day and you are working outside, you may need to come up with ways to hold your signs down. Still, many clubs now have a rally course ring set up in their training buildings for practice. If you meet up with friends to train, you can take turns being responsible for making and setting up a course. Rally signs and holders are much easier to lug around than agility equipment!

325

How to Play 3

Competing in rally does require some training effort on your part. You will need to learn the different signs and their meanings. Your dog may need to learn some new skills or refresh old skills. Still, this is one of the easiest of dog sports to work your way into!

Most rally organizations have three basic levels: a Novice or Beginner level, an Advanced or Open level, and an Excellent or Masters level. In the APDT, the levels have numbers such as Level 1, Level 2, etc. All of the organizations start out with the dogs on lead. This makes it simple to start in competition because no matter how distracted your dog becomes, he is attached to you.

As dogs move up in levels, low jumps may be required, and the dog will need to work off lead—although still with plenty of verbal encouragement and praise from you—and in some organizations you may even progress to retrieving. The APDT is the only organization that allows you to carry a food treat, and the treats can only be given in certain situations. Still, you can have food treats available to reward your dog liberally while training, or you may choose to stop for a quick game with a toy during training.

Rally Speak

Stationary exercises require your dog to stop. The number of stationary exercises that are included on a course are regulated by the different rally organizations.

Rally Stations

The rally signs designate exercises or *stations* where you will be required to perform the action they describe.

Stationary and Moving Exercises: There are generally two types of stations beyond the Start and Finish signs. These are stationary and moving exercises. Stationary exercises require your dog to stop—either in a *down*, *stand*, or *sit*—as part of the exercise. Moving exercises may include change of pace, changes of direction, and maneuvers such as circles. Your own footwork is a factor for many exercises, including both stationary and moving ones. When you stop or halt, your feet need to come together, and unless otherwise stipulated, stay together in place. For some of the three-step exercises, *you* need to do the footwork correctly to help your dog earn full credit for the exercise.

Cone Exercises: Some people break rally exercises down even further—adding a third category—the cone exercises. These exercises include the Serpentines, Weaves, and Spirals. All of them utilize cones as markers for the path you and your dog need to take. It helps to practice with cones so that you learn to judge how much space to leave to keep your dog from knocking any cones over. Plus, you want your dog to be familiar with cones because they will appear on some courses. You don't want him to suddenly notice the cones and try to retrieve or play with them. And yes, I have seen that happen!

Depending on the organization, a course will be required to have a certain number of both types of exercises. A good rally judge will then combine the stations to create a smoothly flowing, fun course. The ideal course takes into consideration that both large and small dogs may be participating, and leaves plenty of space for even giant-breed dogs. If an exhibitor with a disability is

This APDT Level 1 course looks inviting to a beginner.

entered, the judge may make adjustments to allow more time for an exhibitor who moves slowly or to provide extra space for a wheelchair.

In AKC Rally®, a novice course will have 10 to 15 stations (not including the Start and Finish signs). Of those 10 to 15 signs, there must be at least three but no more than five stationary exercises. The APDT has 18 to 20 signs for Level 1, not counting the Start and Finish or any Bonus exercises. In the CARO, the novice course has 20 to 22 signs, including the Start and Finish. Again, it has a maximum of five stationary exercises. The CKC and WWKC require 10 to 15 signs, not counting the Start and Finish, and with no more than five stationary exercises.

Types of Signs

So as you can see, in rally competition, the number of signs and types of exercises required varies widely. To be prepared, you and your dog should be comfortable with all of the basic Novice and Level 1 signs before you enter a trial. While training, be sure to mix up stationary and moving exercises to keep your dog's interest high.

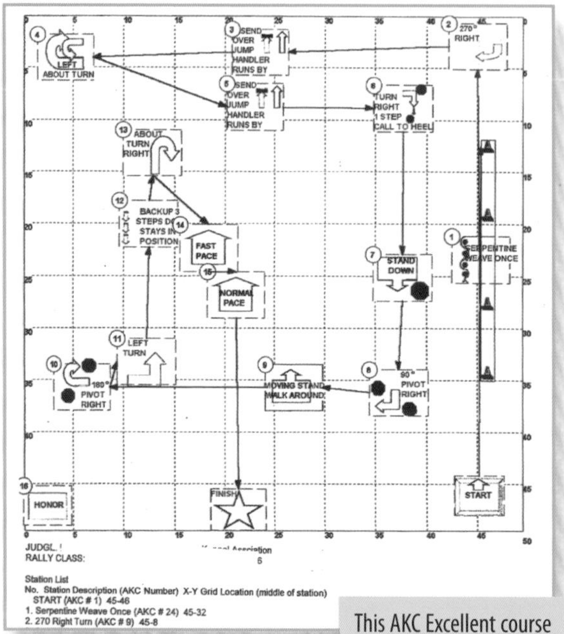

This AKC Excellent course map can look quite intimidating at first.

In the Advanced and Excellent courses in the AKC and Levels 2 and 3 in the APDT, your dog will be required to work off lead and to go over small jumps. (The APDT makes allowances for dogs with disabilities who may not be able to jump safely.) The stations require more precise work on the part of your dog and you—including your own footwork. The APDT often combines signs to allow for mini parts of obedience exercises to be incorporated into a course. You really need to be awake and aware to run a Level 3 APDT rally course—don't skip your morning coffee before those runs!

The Rules

There are similarities and differences among the various rally venues. We will discuss the AKC and APDT, and suggest that you check the rules for the CKC, WWKC, CARO, UKC, and ASCA if you choose to compete in those venues. The AKC and APDT are the two most popular rally venues in the United States, so these are the organizations that will be covered in this book. You will find that if you learn the rules for those two organizations, you will be well prepared for rally anywhere. (By the way, the AKC has now changed the rules for its rally, agility, and obedience competitions, so mixed breeds can now compete there as well as purebreds.)

Elimination

Virtually all dog sports will eliminate a dog who acts aggressively toward another dog or a person—either in the ring or even outside the ring but on the grounds of the trial. Severe corrections given to the dog by you can also lead to elimination. The APDT is stricter on this than is the AKC, and harsh verbal or physical corrections may lead to elimination.

Barking and whether or not to penalize this with points off or elimination is somewhat up to the judge's discretion. Certainly, a dog who barks nonstop while working is likely to be eliminated. A dog who has been debarked but goes through the barking motions should be similarly penalized. Many dogs will bark once or twice with excitement when they go over the jumps at the upper levels. This generally only results in a small penalty if any at all.

Both the AKC and APDT will eliminate a dog who defecates, urinates, or vomits while in the ring. This requires cleanup, of course, and makes the course more difficult for any dogs to follow. Always allow plenty of time to walk your dog so that he can eliminate before his runs. If your dog should have an accident while on the course, don't feel too embarrassed or upset. It has happened to most of us, even with experienced dogs. Offer to help with the cleanup and then quietly take your dog for another walk.

Virtually all dog sports—including rally—will eliminate a dog who acts aggressively toward another dog or person.

Rally Caution

Although rally is quite similar across organizations, there are some differences in signs and scoring. Be sure that you know the rules and regulations of the venue in which you want to compete.

Retries

Retries of stations are allowed by both the AKC and APDT—with a three-point penalty. The AKC now only allows one retry per station. So if you make a major blooper, it may be worthwhile reattempting the sign to change your 10-point error to a 3-point error. However, if your dog has done something like knock the jump down, you are not allowed to replace the jump and reattempt that. If your dog has simply sat slightly crooked, it may not make sense to redo the exercise, possibly accumulating more points off.

Both organizations will give you a nonqualifying score if you totally miss a station and do not attempt the exercise at all, or if you go off course and do stations in the incorrect order. Agility competitors will sympathize with you over the "off" or wrong courses. If you pass a sign but catch yourself before you do the next sign, you can double back. Otherwise, it is too late.

The Walk-Through

A ten-minute walk-through is required by the AKC and APDT for the exhibitors to walk the course and familiarize themselves with the stations and the flow. With a large entry, the walk-through may be split so that you can check out signs and figure out your path without dodging a large crowd. The judge will do a briefing to cover any unusual conditions and answer any questions. Some judges will also have a standard printed briefing that may be available with your course map or posted near the ring.

When you walk the course, you may want to carry your course map with you. Generally, exhibitors are given a copy of the course map when they pick up their arm band numbers. The first time through, make sure that you find each number and get a feel for the flow of the course. The second time through,

The judge watches this team start out nicely together.

actually read each sign carefully. You may even want to perform the sign as if your dog were with you. Don't worry about looking silly—many of the other exhibitors will be doing the same thing. Read the signs carefully. When you get up into Advanced and Excellent, one of the challenges of the course might be to make sure that you do the correct Recall sign. These signs are *very* similar!

With a fairly large dog, look at the moving exercises and try to plan where you will start the exercise so that your dog has plenty of room. Look outside the ring too—to identify any major distractions such as a lunch cart where hot dogs will be cooking.

Timing is done by both organizations. The APDT has a four-minute maximum time unless additional time has been granted due to a handler or dog disability modification. (Those disability forms must be turned in ahead of time so that the judge is aware of the situation.) Time is used to break ties in the AKC, but there is currently no maximum allowed time. This may change in the future.

Ring Size

An AKC Rally® course is set in a ring that measures from 40 x 50 feet (12 x 15

Rally Profile

George and Jake

George and Jake are a dynamic 4-H team. George is the human half of the team—a teenage boy—and Jake is a young Border Collie. George was a somewhat reluctant rally trainer at first. Agility is the true first love of both George and Jake, and they felt rally might be boring. Still, they were willing to try.

The Chow Hounds 4-H club decided to start with APDT rally because mixed breeds could also compete, and the organization was very open to a 4-H club holding some trials. So George decided that he would try to earn a Level 1 rally title through the APDT. Despite being somewhat "forced" to do rally, George did find that both he and Jake enjoy it. "Jake and I like that I can talk to him and help him if he needs it when we compete and train." For Jake, the heeling was a natural behavior, so they had little trouble getting that down pat. Learning some of the unusual turns and working on *stays* took a bit more effort. George also had to learn to be very careful with his lead, as tight-lead points can add up quickly!

While working on a rally title, George and Jake ventured into obedience as well. They have only competed in Pre-Novice but have done quite well. Working in rally and doing the various exercises has improved Jake's heeling. The turns and pivots tend to improve many obedience moves.

George's advice to anyone thinking of trying rally is, "Go ahead and try it! It will help your dog learn to work in new places, and you can talk and help your dog almost as if you were training."

m) to 50 x 60 feet (15 x 18.5 m). The APDT requires more space and stipulates a ring of approximately 50 x 80 feet (12 x 24.5 m). For an indoor trial, the course may have to work around pillars or posts. Outside, you might want to note areas of "dipped' ground, any holes, or any wet areas.

Scoring

AKC scoring begins with the perfect score of 100, with a qualifying score of 70 required. Points are deducted for faults. Faults include doing a very crooked *sit* or a dog who forges way ahead or lags way behind (causing a tight lead) or not performing an exercise correctly. For the APDT, dogs begin with a perfect score of 200, with a 170 required to earn a qualifying leg toward a title. The APDT also incorporates bonus stations for some courses. You are not required to do the bonus, but you can add a possible 10 points to your score if you do it correctly.

Eligibility

Until recently, only AKC-registered dogs—either with full AKC papers or via the ILP (Indefinite Listing Privilege) or PAL (Purebred Alternate Listing) programs could compete in an AKC Rally® trial. As of April 2010, mixed-breed dogs who are registered with the AKC through the Canine Partners program can compete in AKC Rally®. The APDT allows all dogs—including mixed breeds and disabled dogs. Dogs must be registered with the APDT to compete. If the dog has a disability, such as vision problems, a form stating this needs to be filed at the trial in case the judge needs to modify part of the course or an exercise for that dog.

Rally Titles

AKC

Novice Level → RN for Rally Novice
Advanced Level → RA for Rally Advanced
Excellent Level → RE for Rally Excellent
Above and Beyond → RAE for earning qualifying scores at ten trials on the same day in Rally Advanced B and Rally Excellent B. For each multiple of ten that this occurs, it is added to the RAE title, e.g., RAE2.

APDT

Novice Level → RL1 for Rally Level 1
Advanced Level → RL2 for Rally Level 2
Excellent Level → RL3 for Rally Level 3
Above and Beyond → There are championships at each level given by earning ten scores of 170 or better. These are designated as RL1X, RL2X, etc. The APDT also offers ARCH titles for APDT Rally Championships. These are designated as ARCH, ARCHX, and ARCHEX. For each level, the dog-and-handler team must earn 100 Championship points. The number of points is based on scores; for example, a score of 200 equals ten Championship points. For ARCH, the team must earn at least 30 points each for the R1 and R2 levels. It must also have at least five double qualifications (passing in both R1 and R2 at the same trial) with scores of 190 or better in both classes. For ARCHX, the team must have an ARCH title and must also earn ten triple qualifications with scores of 195 or better in all three classes (R1, R2, R3) on the same day. Once past the first ten triple Qs, the team can add designations for each additional ten to be designated as ARCHMX2, for example. For the ARCHEX, the team must have an ARCHX plus earn an additional 10 double qualifications in R2 and R3 on the same day with scores of 195 or better. As additional titling for dogs who may not be able to handle a full APDT rally course, the APDT offers a Puppy Rally title or RLP for any dog earning three puppy scores of 170 or better and a Veteran or RLV title for senior dogs earning three scores of 170 or better.

Judging Guidelines

The APDT is a bit stricter on its judging guidelines. No luring is allowed, so you can't pretend to have food in your hand to help guide your dog around. It is also stricter on harsh commands or corrections, such as leash pops. You are allowed to use food in the APDT, but it must be carried discretely in a pocket and only given to the dog at the end of stationary exercises. Always check with the judge if you plan to carry food, to be sure where and when you are allowed to treat your dog. Use treats that are quick and easy to eat and that won't leave crumbs to distract other dogs.

In AKC Rally®, although you can use treats in training, you are not allowed to carry treats into the ring when competing.

Beyond Organized Rally

Once you move beyond organized rally, anything goes. Stations may require silly and fun actions like singing happy birthday to your dog, or a freestyle-based course may ask for leg weaves or spins. Some fun courses mix in agility equipment with rally signs. The judge may plan a simple veteran dog course and have no *sits*—just moving exercises. Judges can also add interesting variations to the regular rally exercises. Our 4-H has a pair of silly stuffed trucks that make a lot of funny truck sounds (siren, revving engine, etc.). These are often used as part of the Off-Set Figure 8, with someone squeezing the truck to start the sound effects just as a dog approaches.

With the rally format, the sky is the limit for fun and interesting variations!

Skills and Basic Training to Start

4

Although novice and beginner dogs can be successful at rally competitions, most dogs will need some basic training to run a course. Remember that the beginner levels are all on lead, so that makes it easier for young dogs or dogs just starting formal training.

Positive Training

The primary buzzword for rally should be "fun." You want the whole rally experience, from training to competing, to be fun for both you and your dog. Positive training techniques tend to be the most successful and the least stressful for both of you. Using positive techniques, you help your dog do the correct action and then praise, click, treat, or play with him to reinforce that what he did was what you desired. Many trainers start by making it almost impossible for the dog to be wrong. That way, the dog will get plenty of positive reinforcement.

Positioning is one such technique. Using this technique, your dog is kept on a very short lead so that he can't forge way ahead or lag way behind. *Luring* is another positive technique. With this method, you use a food or toy lure to lead your dog into the correct position and keep him there. Clicker training uses a small noisemaker to indicate to your dog that he has performed the correct action, and then you reward that action with a treat, praise, or play with a toy, like a Nylabone. All of these techniques rely on you to recognize when your dog is correct and give him some indication that what he did is what you wanted. Your timing must be impeccable so that you reward the correct action—not the ear scratch that followed the lovely *sit*! Gradually, you can fade out the obvious cues, such as the lure.

With positioning techniques, Kate uses the lead so that Queezle has to stay in position.

Basic Commands

Your dog will need to learn several basic commands for the Novice level: *sit*, *down*, *stand*, *stay*, *recall,* finishing or returning to *heel* position, and walking on a lead without pulling ahead or lagging behind. You may physically help your dog into the *stand* position, but no hands can help for the *sit* or the *down*. These are all useful commands for the pet dog to know around the house as well.

Some basic rules for training are to work your dog at first in a quiet, calm setting. Make sure that you are not tired or stressed out. You want your dog to associate training with you as a fun and good thing. If you have had a rough day, instead of training, simply go for a walk together or play a game like tug or fetch.

Decide right from the start what you will consider an acceptable version of a behavior. For example, if you want your dog to do a nice, tight *sit*, don't reward a sloppy *sit*. Set your standards, and be clear about what is needed to earn a reward. Make sure that you immediately mark that correct behavior with a click or a verbal cue, such as a "yes," said with enthusiasm. Follow that marker with the treat, like a Nylabone, play, or petting that your dog enjoys.

Training Guidelines

- Only train if you are well rested and have a positive attitude.
- Make your training times short and fun. Three or four five-minute sessions are generally better than one half-hour session, especially with a puppy.
- Be very clear, consistent, and concise in what you want from your dog.
- Remember to go heavy on the praise, petting, and play as well as treats.
- If your dog tends to get chubby, use some of his daily food ration as training treats.

Your dog will need to learn several basic commands for the Novice level, including the *down*.

- Some dogs will respond better to hand signals than to verbal commands, so try both.
- If your dog truly resists a certain position, have him checked by your veterinarian to be sure that he doesn't have a medical problem that might make certain positions or movements painful for him. Once your dog is responding to the verbal command, fade away the lures and use your rewards—food, play, or praise—in a random pattern. Think of dog training as having four "Rs": restraint—the stationary positions like *sit* and *down*; resting—the *stays*; return—or *recall* when the dog comes to you; and repeatability—that the dog perform these functions in different settings and under different conditions.
- Never give a command you can't back up. For example, if you are in the shower and your dog walks in, don't tell him to sit unless you are prepared to step out of the shower and help him if he doesn't.

Sit

The *sit* command is useful for helping your dog behave when company comes over, while waiting at curbs for traffic to clear, when brushing his teeth, when cleaning his eyes or ears, and during grooming. Use the *sit* (and all commands you train) in everyday life as much as possible so that they become second nature to your dog.

Most dogs learn to sit on command very early on. Even eight-week-old puppies can quickly pick up this exercise. The easiest way to start is to hold a small treat above your puppy or dog's nose. Raise the treat up, and most dogs automatically go into a *sit* because this raises their heads. As soon as his bottom hits the floor, praise and give the treat. Patience is essential. Also, be sure that you are working on a good surface. A slippery floor may make your dog slide, and he may not be able to sit easily. Carpet, grass, and matting are generally good surfaces for training.

For a small dog, it may be easiest to teach this command up on a table. Follow the same guidelines, but save your back! The same rules apply to using the table; make sure that the surface is not slippery, and be prepared to reward right away. Never leave your dog up on a table alone—jumping down could easily lead to injuries.

Once he is following the lure easily, start adding in the word you want to use for this action. While most people choose to say "Sit," some use more original words or even foreign languages to make their commands unique. For example, some dogs sit to "platz" in German or "plant it" just to be different. Just make sure that you pick one word or phrase and stick with it. The whole family needs to agree on and use the same words to keep your dog from getting confused.

Kate lures using a treat above Queezle's head to encourage her to sit.

Success!

Rally Caution

I often see people shouting, "Sit down you stupid dog!" at their dog who stands there, slowly wagging his tail, not sure if his trainer actually wants him to sit or down. Use the same words for an action consistently, and don't mix them.

Consistency is very important in dog training.

If your dog jumps up instead of sitting, you are raising the treat too high or too fast. Simply close your hand over the treat and do not give it to him. Then start over. You may have to move the lure back behind his head just a bit if he is having trouble getting the idea of the *sit*.

Once your dog is responding to just the word "sit," you may want to add in a hand signal as well. Most people use the left hand coming up, with the palm up, as a *sit* hand signal, but again, you can come up with any signal you want. Simply combine the verbal and visual signals together for a while, and then you can switch to just one or the other. Some dogs respond better to hand signals versus verbal commands and vice versa. Try both and see which your dog seems to like better. Remember that, for a hand signal to work, your dog must be watching and paying attention. In a rally trial, you can use both the verbal and the hand signal if you want, and using both cues also helps keep your dog interested in training. Remember, you want training to be fun and exciting—you don't want him to get bored.

Down

The *down* is another useful command around the house and in real life. Your dog can lie down near the dinner table so that he feels included but is not begging. He can lie down quietly at your feet while you read or watch television. At the veterinary clinic, he can lie by your feet in the waiting room.

The *down* command can be difficult for some dogs. Going into the *down* position can be stressful for a fearful dog because this puts him in a very vulnerable position. It may irritate a dog who is somewhat dominant and doesn't want to appear subordinate to you. Ideally, you have rolled your puppy

George shows Jake a really good treat.

Jake starts to drop down a bit.

Finally—a full drop!

Rally Speak

You will need a *release* command for your dog. This tells the dog that the stationary exercise he has just performed is over now, and you are moving on. For example, after a *sit* and *stay* while you walk around, once you return to the *heel* position, you need to let him know that he is done and can move. Many people use the term "Okay."

over and gently rubbed his belly from the day you got him and done the same to adult dogs, who often enjoy a good belly rub or scratch. This accustoms a dog to assuming a subordinate position while receiving positive feedback and will help make the *down* position a comfortable one for your dog.

Luring is a good way to teach the *down* command. For this training, a slippery floor can be an asset. Have your dog sit because he already knows this—then, take a treat, like a Nylabone, and go from in front of his nose, down and back between his front legs. Most dogs will simply slide into a *down* position. Once he is down, he gets the treat.

This can be done from a *stand* as well. (See the section on "Stand.") Again, with your dog standing, move a treat from his nose, down, and back between his front legs. Many dogs will "fold back" into a nice *down* position. With a small dog, this is another nice place to use a table to train, using the same techniques.

For a dog who truly resists going down, your best bet may be to use a clicker to mark any time he chooses to lie down on his own. Let's face it—sooner or later, every dog lies down to rest! When he does, click to mark the correct behavior and then deliver a treat—to be given while he is lying down.

Once your dog is lying down, either with the lure or the clicker, start adding in the word you want to use. Most people use "down" or "lie down." You can easily throw in a hand signal once your dog understands this word, too. Most people use an overhead hand, moving downward—sort of like a baseball pitch.

Stand

A *stand* is another useful command for around the house. A dog who will do a *stand-stay* can be easily groomed or bathed. He will be easier to rub off with a towel after being out in the rain, snow, or mud, and you can easily dry off his feet while he is standing. Your veterinarian will appreciate a dog who stands while she does the physical examination.

Stand would seem like a very easy thing to teach your dog. After all, dogs stand around all the time. But your goal is to get your dog to stand on command and remain in a *stand*, and that can be trickier. Go back to your basic command: the *sit*. Once your dog is sitting, use a lure in front of his nose to bring him forward. He will reach with his neck and eventually come up to a *stand*. Give him the treat and tell him how clever he is.

Once your dog knows these three basic commands—the *sit*, *down*, and *stand*—make a game out of practicing them. We call it "puppy push-ups" or "puppy drills." Using top-notch treats, like Nylabones, have your dog zip through a *sit*, *down*, *stand* sequence two or three times. Many dogs find it a fun game to beat you to the next position. This can be especially helpful with a dog who isn't sure about doing the *down*. He will quickly learn that a fast drop earns a great treat.

Stay

A *stay* is helpful at home, so that your dog can be near you but not in danger of being tripped over or stepped on. A well-behaved dog who will sit or down-stay quietly is welcome in many homes when you visit.

Learning to stay can be very hard for some dogs, especially young, active dogs. It is best to work on *stay* in very small increments. For a start, the *sit* is often the best command to begin with. For this, make sure that your dog is sitting on a nonslip surface. You don't want him trying to stay but slowly sliding on a slippery floor!

Start by telling your dog to sit. You may want to use both a hand signal and a verbal command for the *stay*. I say "Stay" and put my hand, palm spread, in front of his face. The physical blocking by the hand reinforces the *stay*. If he stays for even a second, praise and release.

Kate uses a hand signal and a tasty treat to get Queezle to stay.

Initially, you will move right in front of your dog as you say "Stay." That way your whole body will act as an additional block to him. Once he is steady with you in front, move to his side or start to gradually move a bit away from him in front. Some dogs do better if you start *stay* training with you beside them. Try both to see which is easier for your dog.

Once your dog stays for even five seconds with you right beside him, helping him, start telling him to stay and then move directly in front of him to face him. If you started out teaching the *stay* from in front, gradually introduce the side position. Gradually build up to about 30 seconds. Be prepared so that if he gets up, you can immediately but gently raise your lead, put him back into a *sit*, and give the *stay* command again. When you train individual signs, your dog will have to stay while you walk around him—and that can be challenging!

When you start to work on those *stay* exercises that require you to move around your dog, do so gradually. At first, say "Stay" and only take one or two steps. Then go back to your original position and praise. Add additional steps slowly as he learns to hold his position even when you move. Remember to keep your lead loose so that you aren't tugging your dog out of his *stay* by accident.

Kate has a treat in her left hand to keep Queezle focused on her and walking with a loose leash.

Recall

Let's face it: The ideal dog would come to a sliding stop while chasing a squirrel, zip around, and barrel back to sit at your feet. That may be hard to accomplish with the average dog, and for dogs with a strong prey/chase drive, it's almost impossible. Still, our dogs can learn to come when called and to be reliable in most situations.

A cardinal rule when calling your dog is that you should never call him when something unpleasant is about to happen. For example, if your dog hates baths, don't call him for a bath. Quietly go and get him. You want him to associate "Fido, come!" with all of the best things in the world—you, a toy, a treat, playtime, etc.

With a puppy or new dog, start by simply establishing his name. Nicknames are cute and many dogs eventually learn to come to a variety of monikers, but to start out, choose just one name. When you say his name, give him a treat, praise, or petting. Eventually, he will turn to look at you as soon as he hears his name and maybe even come. Make sure that you celebrate *every* time he comes to you.

Once your dog is orienting to you, start adding your word for *come*. It might be "come" or "front." The actual word doesn't matter; just be consistent. Now, start saying his name and running backward so that he chases to get to you.

Hokey is paying attention and on a loose leash—if he gets ahead of Kate, she will stop.

Always do *recall* work in an enclosed area. Once you get into a big area, it pays to have a thin line dragging on your dog. Do *not* leave your dog outside with the line on, but when you are out with him, let him drag it around. Periodically call him. If he comes, he gets a treat and a pet and is then sent out to play or explore again. If he doesn't come, gently reel him in. A quick pet, then off he goes again—but no treat, effusive praise, or toy.

Make sure that when your dog is playing in a fenced yard that you do call him and then release him to play again sometimes. Otherwise he will learn that coming when called means the end of playtime.

At first, your goal is simply to have your dog come close enough that you can touch him or his collar, give a treat, and then release him. The final goal is a dog who comes and sits right in front of you. So once he has down the "returning to you" part, use a treat to lure him to a *sit* in front.

For my dogs, I actually use two different commands. "Come" means to come to me, close enough for a touch. "Front" means to come to me and sit directly in front of me—close enough to touch but also sitting very straight. That way, when we are hiking in our fields, I can call "Come" and the dogs know to return to me but that they don't have to sit right in front. That also makes things a bit easier when I am walking multiple dogs so that they aren't all jostling to be the one sitting directly in front.

Heel

For rally, your dog needs to be able to walk along with you on a loose lead and change pace with you. While the exact precision of formal obedience is not required, if you are thinking about going on to obedience, you may want to tighten up the *heel* position right from the start. The ideal *heel* position places the dog at your left side, with his shoulder in a line with your left leg. That description applies whether your dog is a Chihuahua or a Newfoundland. In obedience, even a slight deviation may earn a half-point deduction. In rally, the dog must be farther out of position before any deductions are taken.

However, rally judges are going to be looking for a loose lead, with the lead snap hanging down and no tautness evident. Your dog should not be lagging behind or forging ahead so much that the lead tightens. He should also be

Rally Profile

Lyn, Rowdy, and Tessa

Lyn first became interested in rally back in 2000 when she first heard it proposed. Because no one in her area was doing rally at that time, Lyn started teaching herself and incorporating bits and pieces of rally exercises into her own training. Eventually, Lyn found her way to APDT trials and later on to AKC trials.

Lyn's older male Belgian Tervuren Rowdy has earned an AKC RE and an APDT Level 2 title. Tessa, her young bitch, has worked her way through to an AKC RAE. Lyn enjoys rally so much that she has gone on to become an AKC Rally® judge.

Lyn started doing rally because "I enjoyed it as a break in the training routine. I think it helps strengthen the focus of the dog, and it provides a way to add something different or unexpected into your training." Lyn thinks of rally as a sport itself but also as a pathway to obedience for many trainers. As such, she feels there is too much luring allowed in the AKC. (Note that luring is not allowed in the APDT and will be penalized there.)

Lyn suggests, "If you are interested in rally, find a good instructor. You may also subscribe to the rally obedience list. Signs can be downloaded from the rally list or some organization websites. Cones can be purchased inexpensively at many dollar stores. And then just try it!"

As a judge, Lyn sees some of the same mistakes made time and time again. In Novice, handlers need to be very aware of the tight leash and try to avoid luring if at all possible. Not having good working attention is a problem at all levels. It is a team sport, and your dog needs a solid foundation in basic obedience commands and attention. It is important to know the rules. Not pausing when you walk around your dog is *your* fault, not his, and poor footwork and not training the *stays* can lead to deductions that are handler caused. Lyn adds, "If your dog has truly zoned out, repeating commands often won't help. Instead, back your dog up with you and retry the whole station. Often a fresh approach makes a difference!"

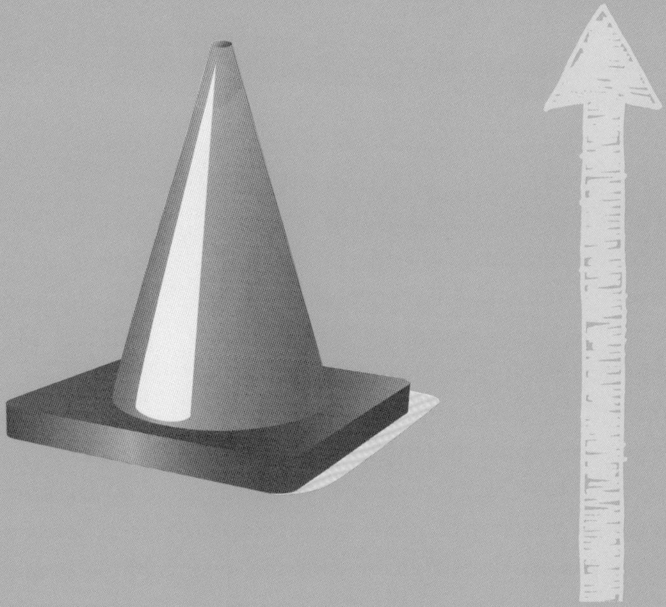

close to your side, not 2 or 3 feet (.5 or 1 m) away.

One of the simplest ways to start working on heeling is to carry a treat in your left hand. The dog simply follows the treat with his nose and his great sense of smell, but he also learns that the *heel* position is a nice place to be. This is basically a lure. Handing out frequent treats is important at first, but gradually wean your dog off. Eventually, you want the treat to be hidden or even left somewhere else and your dog will still heel. If you're using a clicker, click when your dog is in the correct position, then give a treat. Under the section "Attention," we suggest some additional ways to make your dog enjoy the *heel* position.

The ideal *heel* position places the dog at your left side.

Make sure that your dog is only rewarded when he is walking on a loose lead. If he tends to forge ahead, stop the minute he pulls and act like a tree or solid post. You don't need to jerk him back—just stop. He is correcting himself by pulling and by the fact that you aren't coming with him. Most dogs will suddenly stop pulling and turn to look back at you—probably wondering why you stopped! As soon as the tension is off the lead, start forward again. The minute tension comes into the lead, stop again. This is a very good method, but it requires time and patience. It could take you 20 minutes to go the length of a normal driveway with the frequent stops required by a dedicated puller. However, if you are consistent—which means the whole family and whoever walks the dog must play by the same rules—this is a very effective method of getting your dog to walk nicely.

Another way to work on the *heel* position is to have your dog loose in your fenced yard. Start walking around by yourself with a tasty treat in your left hand. If your dog approaches and comes around to sniff the treat, reward him. Put another treat in your hand and continue to walk around. You will find your dog coming over and falling into the *heel* position on his own, hoping to earn those great treats. This will teach his body the correct position, and he will quickly learn to get into that position on lead as well.

The Finish or Return to *Heel*

Once your dog has learned to come and sit in front, you need to get him back to the *heel* position if you want to continue moving through rally stations. Correct *heel* position is by your left leg, with his shoulder right along your pant's side seam. To get back to the *heel* position, your dog must move from sitting directly in front of you to being by your left leg and facing the same direction as you. There are two basic ways your dog can do this. One is by moving to your right and going behind you to come up into his spot. The other way is to turn out and around, or leap up and spin, ending up at your left side. Most dogs (and most people for that matter) end up with a favorite side for the finish, but for rally you must teach your dog both finishes. If you ever go on to regular obedience, you will be grateful that your dog knows both. It also helps to keep your dog's *sits* in front very straight because he never knows which way you may ask him to go next.

Right Finish

For the finish to the right, work on your leash handling. Once your dog is sitting quietly in front, take your leash in your right hand and pass it behind your back to your left hand. Using a lure, place the treat or toy directly in front of your dog's nose with your right hand. Then move your hand around behind you. At the same time, you may apply gentle pressure on the lead. Your dog will ideally get up and move around behind you. As he goes behind, switch the lure to your left hand. Once he is at your side, by your left leg, lure him into a nice straight *sit*.

For rally, you can use both a verbal cue and a hand signal for this action. Most dogs start off needing both but gradually will respond to just one or the other.

Dogs can get distracted while going around behind you—looking at other dogs, any wildlife, food on a nearby table, etc. Luckily, they are on leash at this stage, so you can remind them to move on. Try to encourage your dog to move quickly as he goes behind you because this will give him less time to look for distractions. For many large dogs, the finish to the right is easier than a sharp turn to the left. They are more likely to end up sitting straight when they finish to the right. Still, your dog must learn both, as some rally signs will specify right or left finish.

Left Finish

For the finish to the left, your dog can be lured out and around so that he turns toward you and ends up at your left side. When you first start teaching this, it helps to take a step back with your left foot as you lure him up from his *sit* and out and around. Encourage your dog to actually get up and move to make that turn, as opposed to simply scootching his bottom around.

Once your dog has learned to come and sit in front, you need to get him back to the *heel* position.

Some dogs really prefer to do a leaping touch to your hand and spin in the air to land in *heel* position. This takes an athletic and energetic dog, but some dogs do feel that it is fun to do. If your dog is like this, keep your lure in your hand and raise your hand from his nose, up, back, and out a bit so that he has room to leap and spin. Be prepared for him to crash into you on occasion as he works on both timing and technique.

Choose the Right Words

I always use separate words for the two ways to finish. I want my dog to have as many clues as possible as to which way I want him to go. I use "around" for the right finish and "heel" or "get back" for the left finish. Choose words that are simple and make sense to you. Hand signals for finishing should be done using the hand on the side you want the dog to start moving from—so use the right hand for the right finish and the left hand for the left finish. Initially, you have the leash on, so you can help your dog if he gets confused, but eventually, if you go beyond Novice level (or Level 1) in rally, your dog will be working off lead.

Many dogs quickly learn that they come to you, sit in front, and then go to *heel* position. Some dogs then decide to skip the "sit in front" stage, and this will be faulted by the judge in both rally and obedience. To help keep your dog from anticipating this, it is best not to practice the *recall* and finishes together too often. Instead, to practice a finish, simply tell your dog to sit and stay, then you step in front. Next, give the *finish* command; now your dog won't be connecting it directly with coming and sitting in front. By using both finishes, your dog will also be less likely to anticipate and go directly to *heel*. He knows that he will sit in front no matter what. Then he has to wait for a cue from you as to whether he goes left or right to return to the *heel* position.

Other Pre-Rally Training

Most dogs have picked up *sit* and *lie down* simply from living with their family. To work on advanced concepts, such as *stay* and controlled walking or heeling, your dog will need to focus on you. Working on attention is the best way to gain this focus and help your dog learn to avoid distractions.

Attention

One of the most important things I work on with my dogs is attention. I want my dog to be tuned in to me and responsive to me so that he can avoid distractions and work with me as a team. Much of this work relies on eye contact. I start this with a puppy or new dog as soon as he comes home with me. My pockets generally have some small but tasty treats. (A word to the wise: Dogs are excellent at smelling out treats, so hang your jackets up in a closet or you will find many chewed-out pockets.)

When working with your dog, good eye contact is important.

I touch the dog on the nose (with him sitting if he knows *sit*) using one finger of my hand that is holding a treat. Then I bring that finger to my eye. As soon as he looks at me, he gets the treat. I partner this with a word once he starts to seek out looking at me. I tend to use "watch," but many people use "ready" or "look." Any word will work—just be consistent!

The next step is to have the treat out of sight—often just in your hand by your side. Your dog will nudge the hand, look around, and maybe even whine. At some point, however, he will look at you and make eye contact. At that moment, praise and then treat him. He is learning that checking in with you is a very good thing.

If he is maintaining good attention while in front, try moving to his side and working for eye contact from there too. When you are moving, he will be at your side most of the time. For rally and obedience, your dog will primarily work off your left side. In agility and freestyle, your dog needs to work off both sides. So I try to have my dogs work attention both from sitting at my left side and sitting at my right side. I feel that this equalizes their muscle development as well.

If your dog does not have a *sit* yet, just keep a close eye on him while you are in the house. Any time he looks at you, praise and treat—or click, praise, and treat if you are using a clicker.

Once your dog has what we call stationary attention—neither of you are moving—start training moving attention. In the house, this can be off lead; outdoors, you should be in a fenced area or on lead. With your dog at your side, start to move forward while using your word for attention. If your dog looks up at you, praise and treat. Eventually, you will take more steps away from him before treating, and then you can wean him off treats completely.

Working with your dog off lead in a fenced area, try walking around with a treat in your left hand with it hanging down by your side. When your dog comes over to investigate and falls in step with you, he gets a treat. This is a simplified explanation of the "choose to heel" method of training your dog to walk without pulling. (See earlier section.) Again, your dog learns that being with you, looking at you, and interacting with you is a wonderful and good thing.

A novice dog with good attention and good response to commands like *sit* can actually do a nice rally run without knowing the formal heeling you see in obedience competitions. Many experienced obedience competitors use rally to start their young dogs out so that they get plenty of praise and encouragement without the worry of the precision required for high obedience scores.

Proofing Your Commands

We all know, or have had, dogs who are top stars in their own backyards but who fall apart when out in public. Your dog must be steady despite all kinds of distractions, like other dogs, little kids running by, people with food, etc. So once your dog knows his commands, it is time to take the show on the road.

Do some "proofing" at home. Put toys around where you work or even treats. Then have your dog work while ignoring these distractions. Make sure that the treats *you* have for him are better than those on the floor. If you have children, have them play or throw a ball back and forth. Some people play tapes of dog-show noises or storms.

Try proofing away from home. Many pet stores, farm-supply stores, and hunting-goods stores, as well as some home improvement stores, allow dogs inside. Always make sure that your dog will be good with people—not barking at strangers—before you go into a building. You don't want to ruin the training opportunities for others. And always bring treats and be prepared to back up a few steps in your training at first.

Mall parking lots, as long as the traffic isn't heavy, can be wonderful for practicing footwork and exposing your dog to many distractions and noise. Practice your footwork using the yellow parking lot lines. Going early in the morning before the mall opens is usually a good time for training.

If you are in a formal class, just going to class will expose your dog to other dogs and plenty of distractions. A good teacher will introduce more proofing when the dogs are comfortable working in the class environment.

Rally Classes

There are many ways for you to become trained in rally. Most people find that the easiest way is to sign up for classes at a local dog obedience school or club. Committing to a weekly class tends to make you better about practicing and doing your homework. A class setting provides other people to network with and share training tips with, and it provides your dog with some distractions. For those in northern climates, a class can provide a place to train indoors during the winter. For those in southern climates, a class may provide air-conditioned comfort during the hot months.

Finding a class is usually easy. Ask friends who have trained their dogs where they went. Veterinary clinics and pet stores may suggest referrals as well. (See also Chapter 1.)

Look for an instructor with whom you feel comfortable. If possible, try to sit in on a class to observe. Watch to see if the people and dogs are engaged and having fun. The instructor should be positive and encouraging, as well as experienced with dogs (and ideally, with the sport of rally itself). If you are thinking about someday competing in rally, ask what rally venues the instructor is familiar with. While many signs and judging requirements are similar, some differences exist among sponsoring organizations.

Think about safety. The class should be in a confined area so that if a dog gets loose, he can't escape into a nearby street. Check the footing for both you and your dog. While many training clubs have to go with the space they can find, a modern building and a well-lit parking area with plenty of spaces is a plus. If you live in an area with temperature extremes, make sure that the building is heated or air-conditioned.

If you find yourself stuck with no classes within a reasonable distance or none that fit into your free time, don't worry. With the exercises described in this book, rulebooks from the organizations you hope to compete under, and a set of rally exercise signs, it's possible to make good progress training alone. But always try to find a training partner if you can, simply because training is often more fun with a friend or family member, and you can critique and help each other.

Remember that training alone removes many of the distractions your dog would have in a class. That can make it easier to teach exercises but can prove difficult when you get to a trial and your dog has lots of other things to check out! Remember that last "R": repeatability. Practice in parks, pet stores—wherever you can safely and legally work with your dog.

Rally Equipment

5

After watching an agility trial, you can be thankful that rally requires much less in the way of equipment, and all of it is easy to transport. This is also an area where your creativity can come in. With careful budgeting and some planning, rally can be a very inexpensive source of fun for you and your dog.

Minimum Equipment

- rulebooks for the venues you chose
- a set of signs for the venue you chose
- some sort of holder for the signs so that you can set a course
- some plastic or rubber cones
- leash, including a 6-foot (2-m) one
- approved collar for the venue where you'll be competing
- training aids, such as toys, treats, etc.

Rally Speak

Your rulebook will not only provide descriptions of the signs and exercises but also give you hints about what judges are looking for and what points are deducted where. This is your rally "bible."

- this book to guide your training
- for advanced work, the three obedience jumps: broad, panel, or high and bar

Rulebooks can often be ordered online for a minimal cost of $2 to $5. Some organizations will also let you download rulebooks directly from their sites as well. Then you can print out the pages you want and need for training. If you are in a rally class, your instructor may organize a group order to get a discount and save on shipping when ordering rulebooks from various organizations.

Signs

Rally signs can be ordered online. (See Resources.) These signs come printed on sturdy paper and laminated. But you can also print the signs out from an online source and do your own laminating, which is often the less expensive alternative. Remember, too, that if you are in a weekly class, you don't really need to purchase your own rally signs unless you want a set for extra practice. If you have a friend who is also interested in rally, share a set. Sometimes dog clubs will have extra sets that members can check out—just like books at a library!

If you get into the "just for fun" rally alternatives, such as freestyle and rally, agility and rally, or "silly stuff" and rally, you will need to make some of your own signs. Sturdy cardstock and lamination extend the life span of any homemade signs.

Holders for signs run from the standard metal wire holders to all sorts of creative alternatives. Bulk oil filters (the plastic ones) can be slit so that a sign slips into the slot and the stem holds the sign up. Regular cones can be used with tape-backed Velcro on the cones and the signs—although it can be a bit disconcerting to walk into a ring full of cones and try to pick out which ones are sign holders and which ones are part of an exercise. In this case, different colors can be helpful.

This is an example of a rally sign, printed off the computer and then self-laminated.

The little wooden stands made for displaying ornamental china plates also work well. With all of these alternatives, be aware that on a windy day you may need to stake the holders down or prop up signs. Training alone, you might even be comfortable with simply laying the signs flat on the floor or ground.

Until you feel comfortable enough to design your own rally courses, ask your instructor for sample courses to set up for practice. Most judges have sample courses available for exhibitors at trials. Your instructor and other experienced rally exhibitors may have kept maps of some of the courses, and you can copy these. Books are also available that have sample courses in them. Most of the rally organizations have one or two sample courses on their websites for you to try.

Cones

Cones are necessary for some of the exercises you will be training, such as the Weaves and Spirals. If you can, start out with at least seven cones. That way, you can set up a course with both a Serpentine (Weaves) and a Spiral in it. Initially, you can get by with buckets on the ground, but cones can be found quite inexpensively. The least expensive cones can be found at toy stores or online

Rally Profile

Joan, Sage, Teasel, and Hawkeye

Joan Meyers lives with a beautiful trio of Bernese Mountain Dogs. She started rally right when the AKC did—literally on January 1, 2005! Her dog Sage was the first Berner to earn an AKC Rally® title.

For Joan, rally is a good sport for dogs who may need some reassurance. "My dogs like knowing that they are right. In rally, I can confirm this for them on the spot." Sage is a dog who does not have a lot of confidence. She was working in Utility and developing anxiety about dog shows—probably because Utility can be quite difficult for many dogs. "One time I was at a trial where rally was in one ring and obedience was in the other. Sage was acting anxious when she saw the obedience jumps in the Utility ring. When we got into the rally ring and she realized what her job was that day, I could feel her relax."

A problem for Joan's Berners is that many courses are not designed for big dogs. Her dogs are quite agile (and do compete in agility), but on occasion there isn't even enough room between the Start sign and the ring gating for her dogs to sit comfortably, considering their body and tail length. As Joan adds, "They really don't appreciate being asked to do tight maneuvers right against the ring gating either."

For a novice exhibitor, Joan offers some excellent advice: "Be sure that you and your dog are ready before you enter a trial. Make sure that your dog knows enough about heeling and is able to pay enough attention to you so that you don't end up dragging him from sign to sign." Joan has clearly followed her own advice, as Sage has an RAE, Teasel has an RE, and Hawkeye has an RE—all AKC titles—and all dogs also have many placements.

Rally cones can be simple cones from a toy store.

through children's sites. For very sturdy, larger cones, check out auto-supply stores. Some dog-supply companies also offer cones for sale.

Leash

A comfortable leash is important for any training you do with your dog. I find leather is best for me, but nice inexpensive nylon versions are available as well. For some of the new rule changes, the 6-foot (2-m) length is required. I personally find that too long to be comfortable for most of my training. I use a 3-foot (1-m) lead for at home and for training, but pack the longer lead for competitions and to practice with occasionally. If you have a small dog, be sure that the leash and snap are appropriate in size and weight for your pint-sized canine.

Collar

Different venues have different rulings on what collars are acceptable in the ring. Be sure to check your rulebooks! All will allow a plain buckle or quick-release snap collar. Some, such as the AKC, also allow training collars. Again, be sure that your collar is comfortable for your dog. Dogs are generally not allowed to wear tags in the ring, so you may need a special collar for training that does not have any ID, rabies, or license tags attached to it.

Rewards

What aids you might need or want for training will vary with the dog. My dogs will all happily train for a dry biscuit, a toss of a ball, some praise, or a scratch behind the ears. Other dogs are fussier and want bigger and better "paychecks." One of my friends trains with a veritable smorgasbord of treats—from pieces of roast beef to homemade peanut butter/liver brownies. Other dogs really enjoy a quick tug play session. Try a variety of techniques to see which one brings out the best in your dog. Many dogs work hardest when the rewards change periodically.

Rally Caution

If you train in a park or other outside area, be sure you pick up ALL of your holders, especially if you are using metal holders or spikes to hold signs steady. Forgotten bits of metal can damage mowers or injure people or dogs.

Jumps

Once you move on to the advanced classes, you will need to purchase or make a set of jumps. Plans are available for making your own jumps both from wood and PVC. For training at home, you can even start with a dowel or pole set up across bricks or buckets (with the height depending on your dog's size). Jumps can also be purchased from dog suppliers. See the Resources section for more information.

You can make your own jumps at home using wood or PVC.

11

Training for Rally-O

START

Basic Rally Exercises: Stationary

The stationary rally exercises take basic training commands such as sitting, lying down, and standing and work them into a specific pattern. In this chapter and the chapters to follow, the signs used by the AKC and the APDT will be used to indicate these exercises. Other than color changes, most signs are the same or very similar for the basic exercises. In addition, in these chapters the "Novice" level, terminology used by the AKC, also refers to those types of exercises found in Level 1 of the APDT unless otherwise noted.

The stationary signs all have at least one step in which the dog must stop moving. What he is required to do once he is no longer moving forward will vary with the individual sign. Stationary signs can be the hardest exercises for you, as the handler. You may have to practice your footwork without your dog. Whenever you halt, you need to bring your feet together. If you trained in a marching band or were in the military, this will be second nature to you. For the rest of us, it's a learned behavior. Once your feet are together and planted, they can't be moved until the exercise is finished—with very few exceptions.

For the AKC, a Novice course will have 10 to 15 stations (that does not include the Start and Finish signs). Of those 10 to 15 signs, at least 3 but no more than 5 must be stationary exercises. The APDT has 18 to 20 signs for Level 1, not counting the Start and Finish or any Bonus exercises. In the Canadian Association of Rally Obedience (CARO), the Novice course will have 20 to 22 signs, including the Start and Finish, with a maximum of 5 stationary exercises. The CKC and the WWKC each require 10 to 15 signs, not counting the Start and Finish, and with no more than 5 stationary signs. So as you can see, in rally competition, the number of signs and types of exercises required can vary widely. To be prepared, you and your dog should be comfortable with all of the basic Novice and Level 1 signs before you enter a trial.

At the Novice level, you are allowed to clap, pat your leg, chirp, sing, talk as much as you want, etc., to encourage your dog. If you give repeated commands you will be penalized, but you have huge latitude in what you can do to help your dog. One thing you can't do in rally is touch your dog, except for the Stand exercise in Advanced and if you need to untangle your lead in Novice.

Stationary exercises are performed with the sign to the handler's right side. The rules say "near" the sign. So figure that you should be at least within 3 to 4 feet (1 m) of the sign—ideally a bit closer. If the exercise requires your dog to go around you to the right, always make sure that you leave enough

space for him to fit. If you have trouble remembering which side that the signs should appear on, think about the fact that your dog is on your left side and you want him on the side away from the signs. To begin with, you don't want him knocking a sign over, and on top of that, *you* need to be able to read the sign. Even clever dogs don't generally read the signs for you!

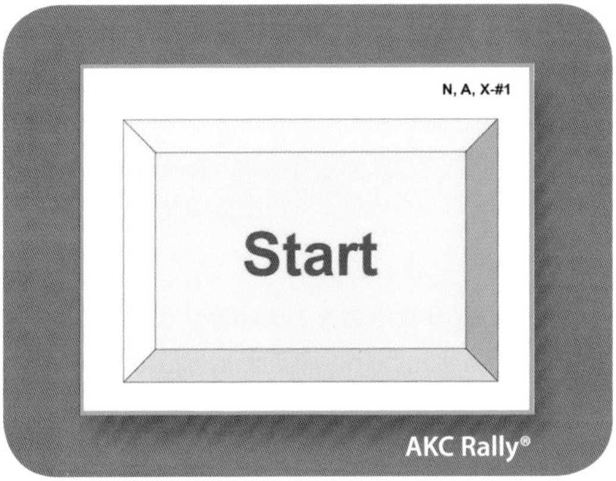

Start

A Start sign is used to indicate the beginning of the course. The dog does not have to be sitting at the start. This sign lets you know where to line up.

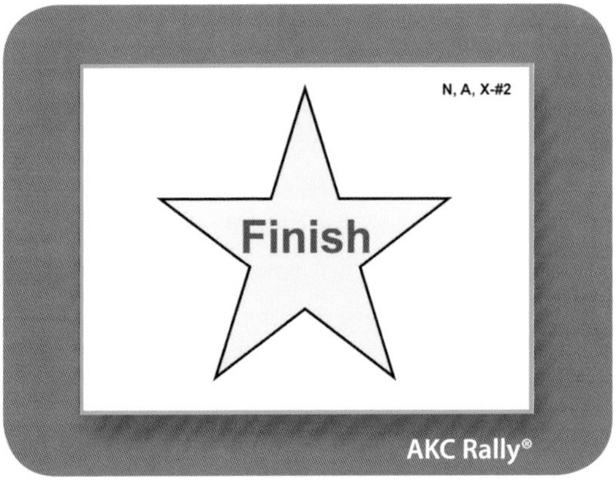

Finish

This sign indicates the end of the course. The course timing stops when your dog passes this sign.

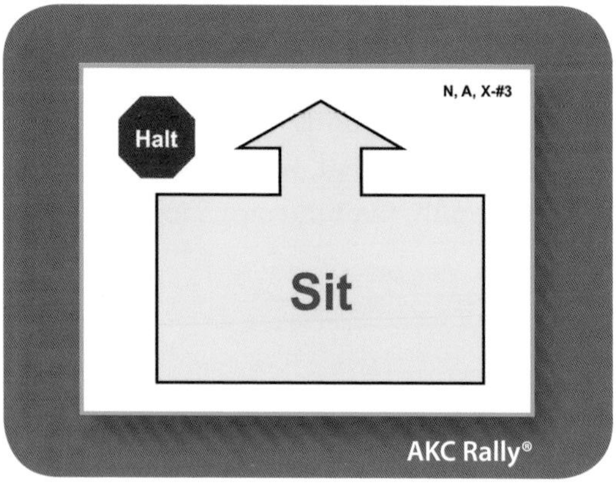

Halt, Sit

The Halt, Sit is a very basic sign using a standard exercise of heeling. You move forward toward the sign, with your dog walking with you on a loose lead, in the *heel* position. When you stop, your dog should sit by your side. Some dogs who have had more obedience training will do an automatic *sit*. If your dog does not sit automatically, you are allowed to give a *sit* command. The command can be a verbal or hand signal, or you can use both.

This is an easy sign to train for. Simply practice whenever you are out walking with your dog under control. When you stop, he must sit. At first, you may have to lure the *sit* (see Chapter 4), but he will quickly learn to associate the word for *sit* with the action. Be sure to praise him!

When you lure or reward, make sure that the treat or toy is directly in front of your dog's face and that his body is straight. Give the treat, like a Nylabone, only if he is sitting straight, facing directly ahead, or with his body straight and only his head turned toward you. Do not reward him if he is sitting sideways, looking at you. If your dog has trouble sitting straight, make sure that your treat or toy is in your left hand so that he isn't curling around in front of you to get closer to his reward. Try practicing in a hallway, right up alongside the wall so that he has to sit straight.

Halt, Sit, Down

The Halt, Sit, Down exercise starts out like the simple *sit* described previously. Your dog moves with you, you stop, and he sits. You now want him to go from his *sit* to a *down* position, without getting up or moving around.

This is another time when first training with a lure may be the easiest. With your dog sitting straight at your side, reach down and place a treat between his front legs but back a little. On a slippery floor, he may just slide into the *down* position. The "foldback down," in which the dog's front legs remain in place but he folds his body back and into the *down,* is the most desirable, but you won't lose any points if he keeps his rear legs in place and inches his front legs forward.

This Malinois shows a nice *sit*, and the handler is indicating a *down*.

The dog must go all the way down—even his elbows—for the *down* to count. Again, you want your dog's body to stay straight if at all possible. Many dogs tend to curl around partly in front of you when they lie down. Leaving your left leg slightly out in front of your body may prevent this when training—just your foot will be plenty to help block a small dog. You can't do this in a trial, however, as your feet need to remain together.

Once your dog is down, pause—even if just for an instant—so that it is clear that your dog is down. I always suggest that my students take a deep breath before moving on. You and your dog then move forward, with your dog going directly from lying down to walking on.

Halt, Walk Around Dog

The Halt, Walk Around Dog sign incorporates a short and simple *stay* with the Halt, Sit exercise. You move forward and come to a halt. Your dog then sits at your side. The *sit* is implied by the halt and the fact that you have a stop sign. Once your dog is sitting, tell him to stay and walk around him, going counterclockwise and returning to the *heel* position.

You may give your dog both a verbal command to stay and a hand signal. You may also repeat the *sit* and the *stay* commands if you need to. At the Novice level, your dog will be on lead, of course. So be careful while walking around not to pull on the lead or to swing the lead into your dog's face. Many dogs have trouble with this at first, especially if you are still luring many behaviors

Kate gives Queezle the *stay* signal as she starts to walk around her.

As Kate walks around, she makes sure that the leash stays loose.

The exercise ends with Kate in *heel* position.

because they want to follow your hand. If that is the case, try keeping your left hand steady, holding the lead near your dog's face. The right hand can be used for the hand signal.

Walk briskly, but not running, as you move around your dog. Return so that your left leg is at the level of your dog's right shoulder. Once you are back in this heel position, pause for an instant. Again, a good way to practice this is to always take a deep breath once you are back in place. You want to be sure that the judge has time to register that you did the required pause.

Rally Speak

Stationary exercises can get boring very quickly for your dog. Dogs like to move, so stationary exercises aren't as much fun as moving ones. Make sure that you mix up this training with lots of fun. If your dog consistently resists a certain position, such as the *sit*, have a veterinary checkup to eliminate the chance of any physical problem.

Halt, Down, Walk Around Dog

This exercise is similar to the previous one. You walk forward and come to a halt. Your dog should sit by your side—use a verbal command or hand signal if you need it. Once your dog is sitting, tell him to lie down. Again, you can use verbal and hand signals. Many dogs respond well to a hand pointing at the floor or ground. Your dog needs to go directly from the *sit* to the *down*—he should not get up or move between the two positions.

When your dog is down, including his elbows, tell him to stay using a verbal and/or hand signal. Then walk around him, counterclockwise, and return to *heel* position. (This is still with your leg even with his shoulder, even though your dog is lying down and not sitting.) It can be even trickier to handle your leash for this. Keep your leash in your left hand, and try to keep that hand steady, holding the leash so that it doesn't hit your dog in the face as you move around. Avoid any tension or pull on the leash.

Once you are back in *heel* position, pause, take a deep breath, and move on!

The next set of signs deals with a Call Front or Recall. In each of these signs, you will move forward, then step back and call your dog to come sit in front. That is the first step for each exercise. Whenever your dog is called to front, he is expected to sit. Then, the second step is getting your dog back into *heel* position so that you can move on to the next

exercise. For these signs, you may need to practice running or at least moving quickly backward for a few steps. It might be a good idea to practice this without your dog at first!

The first set of signs requires your dog go to *heel* position but not sit. Instead, you and your dog move forward as soon as he goes to the position. One way to remember this is that the signs that say "forward" have an "o" in them like the word "go."

Call Dog Front, Forward Right or Call Front, Finish Right Forward

This is the first of the Novice Recall signs. Luckily, in Novice you are allowed to move backward when you call your dog. This helps keep him excited about coming to you and can help with getting him to sit straight in front.

To start, you and your dog move along together, going forward. Then, back up while calling your dog. Ideally, he will turn and follow after you. When you come to a halt, he should sit in front of you. Once he is sitting, give him the command to finish or return to *heel* position. For this station, he must finish by going around you to your right.

To teach this sign, walk briskly forward. Then, give your dog a warning, such as saying his name clearly. Immediately follow that by taking two or three quick steps backward. Your dog should turn to come to you because

Rally Profile

Jean and Tiara

Jean's stunningly beautiful Belgian Tervuren Tiara can also be a handful! From the start, Jean was looking for ways to engage her puppy's busy mind and athletic body. They started out in a puppy class whose instructor was an AKC Rally® judge. The instructor felt that rally was a great way to teach basic foundation behaviors, and she hoped that her students would go on to compete in rally.

For Jean, rally was a great way to start her performance puppy. Tiara loves the fun they have both training and competing because Jean is free to use her voice, move freely, and encourage her with hand motions. Tiara quickly learned the Halt and Sit signs because she was already learning to sit when Jean stopped while heeling. The two performance areas—obedience and rally—overlap there.

Jean feels that "Rally exercises helped to build the foundation for Tiara's learning, confidence, attention, and motivation. She learned to read my body language and improved her own body awareness, such as coordination." Because Jean's goals include high-level titles in obedience and agility, she wanted the best possible start for her canine partner. Many of the rally signs and exercises encourage a dog to be aware of his hind legs, which is important for agility and mimics the "doodling" that top obedience competitors do to keep their dogs enthused and interested in their work.

Since starting her puppy classes, Jean has moved on to competitive agility and obedience classes. Tiara earned her Novice title or RN in the AKC as well as her RA. These titles were earned with high scores and placements. Any concerns that Jean had about rally possibly creating training or showing problems for obedience were dispelled when the team also earned a Companion Dog (CD) obedience title with high scores and placements.

Jean feels that rally is a great sport for many dog-and-handler teams. "It has been a wonderful experience to see so many different teams competing. There are handlers in the past who would have only attempted a CD or were only serious about the breed ring. Now they have embraced rally as a fun alternative, and some are even working all the way through to an RAE!" The rally competitions give the exhibitor more chances to be in the ring.

Jean truly feels that rally gave her and Tiara a great jumpstart on their performance career. "I highly recommend rally to any dog–handler team. It is a wonderful and positive way to spend time with your dog. You both learn more about each other as you journey on your way through life together!" Jean and Tiara are a team to watch for enthusiasm and precision.

Rally Caution

Once you stop on these Recall exercises, your feet must stay in place, planted side by side, until the exercise is done. So while you can use a step back in training to work on your dog's finish to the left, once you are in a rally competition, you may not move that foot. Remember to practice not moving that foot or taking those extra steps before you go to a trial.

he expects good things to happen when he hears his name and/or hears your word for *come*. When he comes, use a verbal or hand signal (or both) to remind him to sit directly in front of you. If you need to use lures, the toy or treat should go in front of your dog's nose as you are walking. Then, bring the lure back to you as you step backward. And finally, the lure comes up in front of your dog so that he sits when he gets to you. A judge will want to see the lead stay loose so that you aren't using it to make your dog turn and come. Next, your dog should sit fairly straight in front of you. (Remember that for the AKC you need to wean off the lures, treats, and toys before you compete because you can't have them in the ring!)

If your dog tends to sit to one side, it may be that you always deliver his rewards from one hand or that you practice going from the front to the *heel* position too often. Some dogs also simply have trouble sitting very straight and tight. Work on straight *sits* in front by using your legs as a chute or using other props to guide your dog into you correctly.

Once your dog is sitting, you now need to get him up and around you. This sign says "Forward," so your dog will *not* be sitting once he gets to *heel* position. Instead, as he starts to move around behind you, you need to start moving forward.

Most dogs think that this is a fun sign, and they quickly learn to zip around you so that they aren't left behind. Do encourage your dog to move quickly so that he doesn't have time to get distracted looking around as he goes behind you.

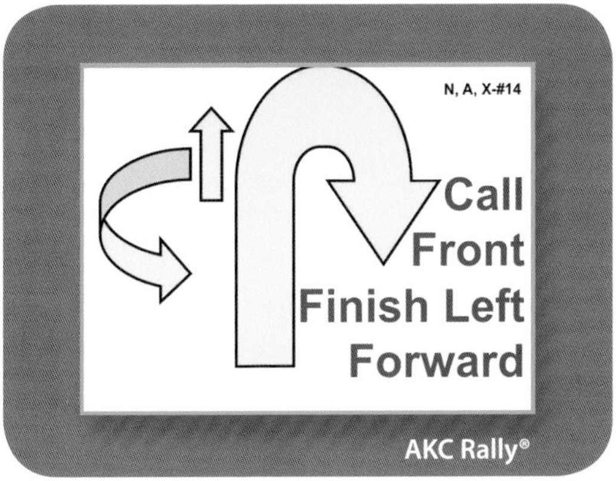

Call Dog Front, Forward Left or Call Front, Finish Left Forward

This sign is very similar to the previous one above except that, after your dog does his nice straight *sit* in front of you, he now has to return to *heel* position by spinning or twisting to your left. To teach this sign, do the *recall* training above to get the straight *sit* in front.

Now, you need to get your dog to your left and turned to face forward. A lure can be used in front of his nose, with your left hand to guide him from in front to out and around by your left side. When luring, it helps to take a step back with your left leg—maybe even two steps if you have a big dog. Athletic, energetic dogs sometimes prefer to actually leap up to touch a raised hand and then spin into place.

Queezle is doing a nice straight *sit* directly in front of Kate.

This sign then says "Forward." This means that you do *not* want your dog to sit in *heel* position. So be prepared to move as soon as your dog heads around to your left.

Two more Novice-level signs combine the Front and Finish. In these cases, the dog will go to *heel* position and sit. You will pause—take a deep breath—and then move on. These signs say Halt and/or have a stop sign to warn and remind you that the dog must sit before moving on.

Call Dog Front, Finish Right, Halt or Call Dog Front, Finish Right

Once again, you need a good *recall*. Remember to warn your dog so that you don't pull on the leash. Most dogs quickly learn to associate your movement backward with the *recall* and Front position.

Walk forward and then step backward, calling your dog to you. The dog will sit in front. Now give your verbal and/or hand signal for the Right Finish. This time, your dog will go around you to the *heel* position, and he should sit. Give a *sit* command when he gets to the *heel* position. Once he is in the *heel* position, pause, then move forward. Always make sure that your dog is sitting before you move on.

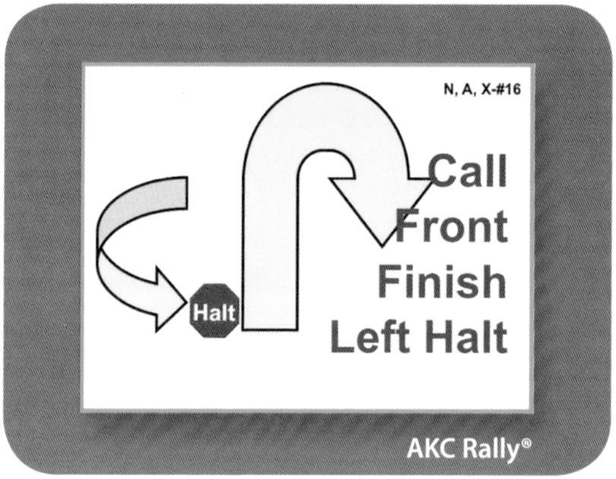

Call Dog Front, Finish Left, Halt or Call Dog Front, Finish Left

This is the last of the four simple *recall* Novice signs. Use your dog's name a split second before you back up so that he knows what is coming. This will also help keep your leash loose. Move forward, then say your dog's name and your *recall* command as you are stepping backward. Stop and your dog should sit in front. Ideally, you want a nice straight *sit* directly in front of you. Once your dog is sitting, give him the verbal and/or hand signal to finish to the left. Remember, in training you can move your left leg back a step or two to help guide your dog back and around. In a trial, however, your feet must remain planted until the exercise is over.

When your dog gets to the *heel* position, you may give the *sit* command or hand signal if you need to. Once your dog is sitting, pause and then proceed.

The next sign is a challenge for the handler—you must do your footwork correctly and your dog must get up and sit straight and facing forward multiple times in a row. Some dogs feel that this is just too much repetition!

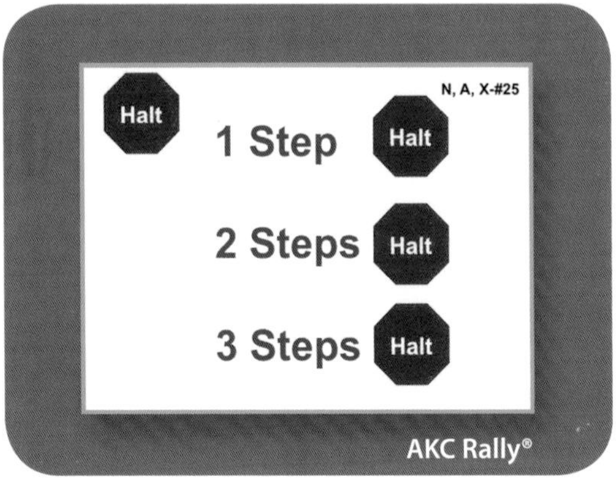

Halt, 1, 2, and 3 Steps Forward

Your job has now gotten trickier. You must be sure that your footwork is correct for this sign. I strongly suggest that you practice this without your dog first!

For this exercise, you and your dog move forward together. Ideally, your dog is at your left side in the *heel* position and on a loose lead. Together, you come to a halt, with your dog sitting at your side, facing forward and body straight. Once you have both stopped, take one step forward while telling your dog to heel. Take just one step, then feet together and halt. Your dog must move just the distance of that one step and then immediately sit again in the *heel* position. Once you are both stopped and your dog is sitting, go forward two steps, put your feet together, and stop. Again, your dog must move with you and then sit as you halt. For the final part of this sign, take three steps, get your feet together, and stop. Your dog should come the distance of the three steps and once again sit in the *heel* position. Once he has done the third *sit*, you move forward as a team.

This sign seems to make more sense for a little dog than for a big dog. The little dog is actually covering some ground and taking multiple steps between the *sits*. A big dog may barely stand up before he has to sit again. With a big dog, you really want to try to take a long stride. Older dogs and dogs with arthritis problems may resist doing the multiple *sits* so close together. This is not an exercise that I would practice multiple times in a row. Even the most tolerant dog will begin to question your wisdom! Make sure that you break up practicing this exercise with plenty of praise, treats, toys, and fun.

The next sign is another test of your footwork. Remember, practice without your dog sometimes so that you can work on your homework without boring him.

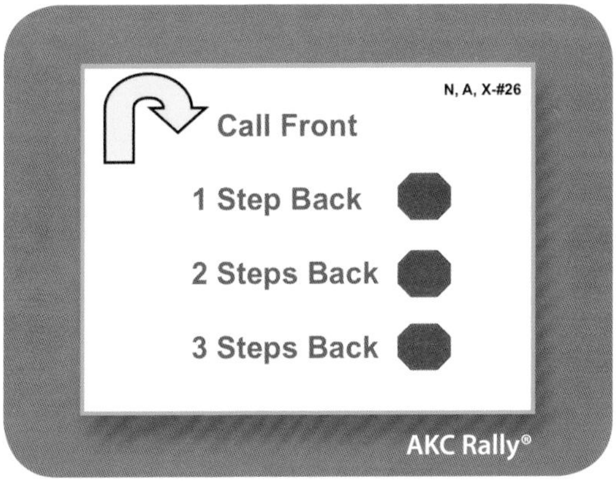

Call Front—1, 2, and 3 Steps Backward

This sign is a Novice sign in the AKC but a Level 2 sign in the APDT. You and your dog walk forward. You then move backward and call your dog into a *sit* in front of you—just like the earlier Recall signs. Once your dog is sitting, take one step back and call him as you move. He should move along with you. When you halt—remember, just one step!—your dog should sit in front again. Now that your dog is sitting, take two steps backward, halting with your feet together. Call him as soon as you move so that he comes with you and once again sits in front. For the final part of this exercise, take three steps backward, calling your dog as you move, halting with your feet together and with your dog sitting in front. For some reason, the three steps backward feel very awkward to many people, so you do need to practice your footwork to be sure that you don't throw in an extra step.

That is a *lot* to keep track of! Remember that you can call your dog and use a hand signal or pat your leg if you need to inspire him to get up and move with you. You can also use a verbal and/or hand signal to encourage him to sit in front. Some dogs find this sort of "scoot Front" action fun. Other dogs will once again question your wisdom at making them get up and then sit again so quickly. Be sure to provide plenty of rewards for this exercise.

You may also need to go back and practice your Fronts—using a leg to guide your dog into place. You are not permitted to do that in a trial, but it can be helpful in practice to reinforce to your dog that you want him straight and in front.

This Corgi is holding the *down-stay* at a trial.

The next sign is a change for the AKC. The old Moving Down exercise was confusing for trainers and judges—and even for the dogs once in a while! It was very difficult for judges to be consistent when scoring this performance, so the AKC modified the exercise.

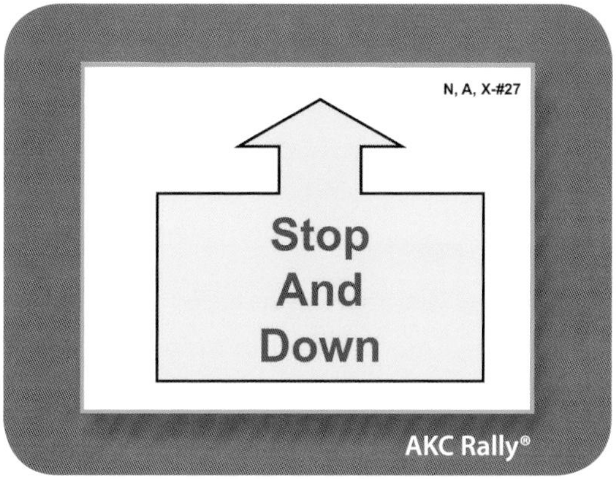

Stop and Down

For this exercise, the dog and handler move forward. The handler tells the dog to lie down. This can be just a verbal cue, just a hand signal, or both. The handler stops next to the dog. Once the dog is totally down—even the elbows!—the team moves forward.

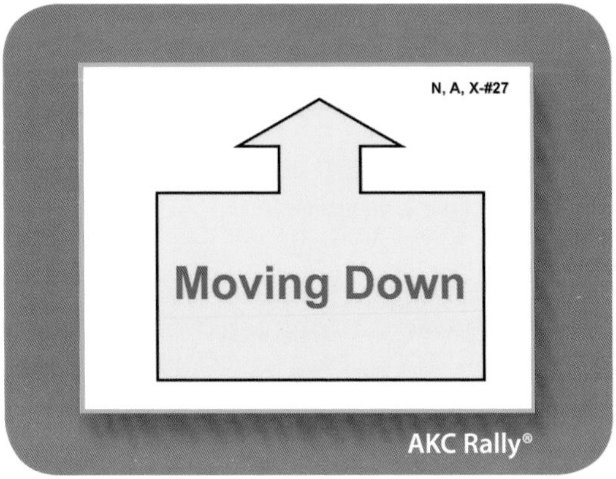

Moving Down and Forward

For the APDT version (a Level 2 sign), the handler tells the dog to down as they are moving forward and may, if need be, step in front of the dog as she signals and/or gives the command. Once the dog is down, the handler returns to heel, and they move on.

There are two key elements here: the dog must lie down all the way, and he must go to the *down* position without stopping and sitting first. If you have taught the foldback *down,* this will be easy for your dog.

Most dogs find doing a quick *down* for a treat very rewarding. Make this a game: Hold an extra-special treat right in front of his nose, then quickly drop your hand to the floor. If he is toy crazy, use a toy instead. Once he is all the way down, take a quick breath, then release him up and into play.

This Rottweiler and her handler prepare to move out from the *sit*.

They move off at an obviously fast pace.

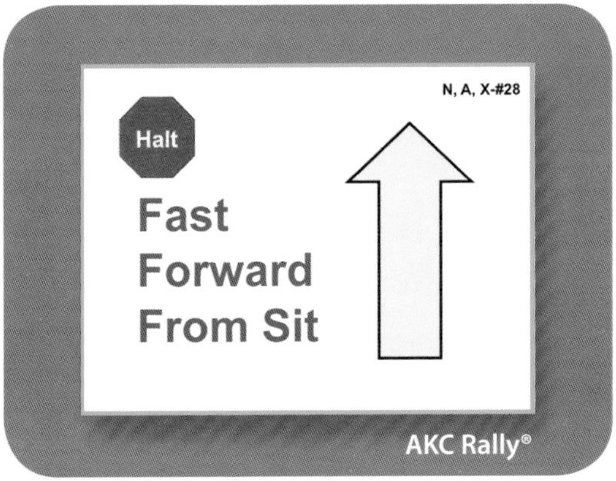

Halt—Fast Forward From Sit

This is an exercise that most dogs like. You move forward with your dog and come to a halt. Your dog should sit at your side in the *heel* position. Once he is sitting, go forward at a fast pace. You can, and probably should, warn your dog that you are about to move off quickly instead of at your normal pace. You want your dog right with you—not lagging behind. In practice, put a hand on his collar and hold him back a bit while saying something like, "Ready, ready, we are going to go!" Then hustle off, leaning forward a bit to encourage him to hustle too.

This sign will be followed by a Normal Pace sign, or it may be used as the last sign of the course so that you hustle along to the Finish sign. Dogs think that this is fun. They look at you and wait to race you as you take off. If this is not the last sign of the course, be ready to straighten your body as a signal that you will be slowing down as you approach the Normal Pace sign.

Basic Rally Exercises: Turns

7

Obviously, you can't spend your entire time on a rally course doing stationary exercises. You need to move about, and as part of that movement, you need to do some turns. Unusual turns are one of the unique aspects of rally, and these include exercises that are designed to keep you and your dog on your toes. A variety of turns will help you both work as a team and sharpen up heeling skills in case you choose to go on to competitive obedience. Many of these moves were originally called "doodling" by obedience competitors.

Turn signs will appear in front of you. In general, you perform a turn sign while standing in front of it—not keeping the sign on your right, as you do with most other signs. For all turns, you and your dog must be moving together, although not always in the same direction. You need to be fluid and smooth, and you may want to work on your footwork without your dog sometimes. That way, when you go to train with your dog, you will be confident and smooth and can help him learn his part of the teamwork.

Especially when you are starting rally, it is a good idea to warn your dog that you are about to do a turn. Use his name or do something to focus his attention on you. If you have an *attention* command (see Chapter 4), this is a good time to use it.

Right Turn

Kate moves her shoulder forward just a little to tip Queezle off that a right turn is coming.

This is a straightforward, right-angle or 90-degree turn to the right. You turn to the right, and your dog turns with you. This puts your dog on the outside of the turn so that he will have to hustle a bit to stay in an ideal *heel* position. Keep your feet under you—not swinging your left leg out as you turn. If your leg swings out, your dog will go wide and end up out of position.

A standard footwork pattern is to plant your right foot. Move your left foot into a "T." Then swing 90 degrees on the right foot and step off with the left foot. You may find a different pattern more comfortable for you. The point here is to develop standardized footwork. Your dog relies on your body language and movements as much or more so than on your verbal commands. By using consistent footwork, you give your dog more clues about what comes next. This will aid him in staying close to you and staying focused on you.

You can also use subtle—note I said subtle!—movements of your shoulder and head to help your dog. Walking naturally, a person tends to look in the direction that she is turning, so it makes perfect sense to do so here. You can also bring your left shoulder slightly forward as you go into the right turn. The shoulder movement will bring your dog forward as he follows your body language.

While this turn is a 90-degree turn, it does not have to be stiff and military. It should also not be a loopy, sloppy turn either. Work for the happy medium. Done correctly, the right turn should end with you heading directly toward your next sign.

If your dog tends to lag on this turn, try throwing a treat or toy ahead of you as you make the turn in practice. This will encourage him to move quickly through that turn.

Left Turn

This is the "mirror" of the right turn. You are now going to turn directly to the left in a 90-degree arc. This time, your dog will be on the "inside" of the turn and will have to slow up or shorten his stride to stay in position. Again, your consistent footwork can help your dog. This time, plant your left foot. Your right foot will form a "T." Then swing 90 degrees on your left foot and step out with your right foot. As mentioned above, look into the turn and where you are heading. Plus, in this case, bring your left shoulder back slightly. This will slow your dog and make him think about swinging his rear end over.

As above, this does not need to be a strict, military-style turn. Still, you want a fairly tight turn, with your dog staying in the *heel* position. Many dogs have a tendency to either forge ahead and sort of crash into your leg or lag behind as you turn. It can help when you practice left turns to put your leash behind your legs so that the leash runs from the dog's collar, behind your legs, and to your right hand. As you turn, the lead acts to lever your dog tightly around to the left.

If this sign is performed correctly, you should now be heading toward the next sign in the correct sequence.

The shoulder cue is exaggerated here to help Queezle learn the left turn.

Rally Speak

Footwork refers to what *you* are doing—how you move your feet, what steps you take, and how you turn.

About Turn, Right

For this turn, you and your dog move forward. The sign comes up in front of you, just like the other turn signs do. This time, however, you and your dog turn to the right to face back the way you just came—a turn of 180 degrees. Because you are turning to the right, your dog will be on the "outside" of the turn and will have to hustle a bit to stay in the *heel* position. Make sure that you leave room for your dog to fit between you and the sign as you turn. Once you have turned, you should see the next sign in the sequence in front of you.

Dogs can lag or fall behind on this turn. Practice your footwork alone. You want to plant your right foot, make a "T" with your left foot, pivot around (180 degrees) with your right foot, and move off briskly. While training, it can help to throw a toy or treat as you come around. Throw this in the direction you are now heading. This will encourage your dog to hurry around you and stay in the *heel* position. Remember to look in the direction you will be turning and then going. Also, ease that left shoulder forward a touch to cue your dog that the turn is coming and which way you plant to go. This turn is usually easier for most teams than the following turn.

About "U" Turn

Once again, you and your canine partner will be turning to head back in the opposite direction, but you will turn to the left. This puts your dog on the "inside" of the turn. He needs to slow down, shorten his stride, or even possibly take a step or two backward to remain in decent *heel* position.

Your footwork will be to plant your left foot, make a "T" with your right foot, pivot 180 degrees on the left foot, and step out briskly with the right foot. Look in the direction you are turning and to the direction you plan to go. Move your left shoulder back a touch to give your dog that extra cue that you are turning left and that he needs to slow down and move back a bit. This is another turn that can be practiced with the lead running behind your legs.

The next set of turns tests your geometry skills from high school. You will be doing 270-degree and 360-degree turns. I find it easier not to worry about the exact degrees and angles. Concentrate on where you will need to go next, and if all else fails, simply follow the drawing on the signs. These turns do not have to be as tight as pivots, but they should not be much wider than a hula hoop—and even that size should be reserved for large dogs.

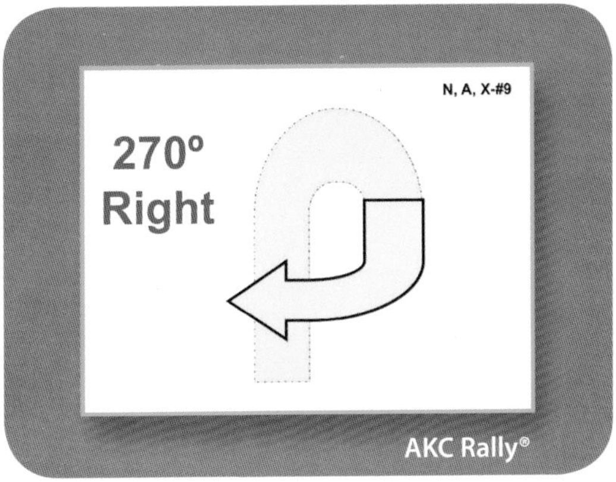

270-Degree Right Turn or 270-Degree Right (Turn)

For this turn, move forward as a team with your dog. You will turn to the right, so your dog needs to hustle again. Continue on with your turn until you have turned so far that you are now moving left from where you started. Make sure that you leave room for your dog to fit between you and the sign as you turn together. A 270-degree turn will always take you in the opposite direction as it is listed. So in this case, the 270-degree *right* ends up being a fancy way of doing a *left* turn. Most dogs like these because they spin around with you. This does not have to be a tight pivot-type turn, but it should not go extremely wide either. Dogs tend to perform these turns fairly tightly. You will need your right-turn cues again—slight movement of the left shoulder forward and possibly tossing a toy or treat while training.

When in doubt or on days when your mind is blanking out on the "degrees," simply follow the drawing on the sign. When walking the course, make sure that you know where the next sign is after each turn. If you finish the turn correctly, you should be lined up for the next number in the sequence.

Rally Profile

Brenda, Tae, and Mace

Brenda was at a dog obedience match when she got the chance to watch rally back in 2002. As she says, "I was hooked because the exhibitors and their dogs were having so much fun." At that time, the APDT was already running titling rally trials, so Brenda jumped in with both feet (and eight Rottweiler feet too!).

Brenda competes in obedience and agility,as well as rally, wanting her dogs to be well rounded. For her, a major plus to rally is being able to take a young dog into the ring environment, with all of its stresses and distractions, but being able to help them get used to the routine of showing and competing. In the APDT, you can even use food at certain times, which can be especially motivating for puppies.

For Brenda, training in rally has been a win–win situation. "Rally has helped in all areas of training, even agility. I think it reinforces the basics, which I tend to be a stickler for. I like to take training in little steps, and rally really focuses on those steps." Brenda's dogs are extremely successful in obedience, rally, and agility, so her hard work has paid off!

The hard part of doing rally as well as other sports is for the handler to remember not to give extra or double commands when it is not allowed, such as in many obedience exercises. Still, the "handler problem" is worth it for the increased precision and motivation of the dogs. Some rally exercises require very meticulous footwork (on both the part of the handler and the dog) and a definite teamwork type of rhythm. The Back Three Steps exercise is a good example of that and can be difficult for a large dog to master.

Tae and Mace are both very fit and athletic dogs. They love to jump, and while the rally jumps are low, they are still fun. What can be difficult is fitting the big jumping stride of a large male Rottweiler to the usual rally ring and getting the dog's attention back after the fun of jumping. The low jumps are a good starting point for a dog heading for upper-level obedience and/or agility.

Brenda has now competed at upper levels in both APDT and AKC rally, garnering many trophies, placements, and awards along the way. She feels that the APDT, especially once you reach Level 3, is a nice preparation for Open and Utility obedience work. It has certainly paid off for her!

For a novice thinking about trying rally, Brenda offers this advice, "Go for it! Just prepare yourself by learning the signs and knowing how to correctly execute the exercises. I suggest finding an experienced teacher who has competed in rally at least to the Excellent level."

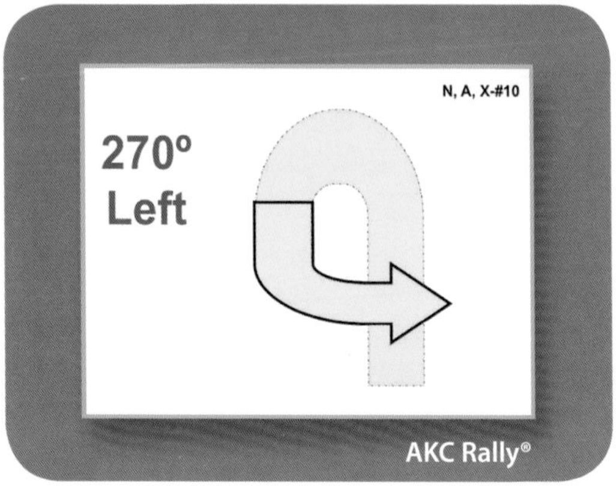

270-Degree Left Turn or 270-Degree Left Turn

This is the mirror of the above sign. You now head forward and turn to your left. This means that your dog must slow up or shorten his stride. You continue on the left turn until you end up going to the right (based on the direction you were originally heading.) This is another turn you may initially want to train with your leash behind your legs.

Shoulder cues—in this case, moving your left shoulder back just a bit—will help cue your dog that he needs to slow down or back up. This turn does not have to be a tight pivot, but it shouldn't go very wide either.

When you walk the course, check to be sure that the turn finishes correctly—lining you up for the next exercise in the sequence. If you feel confused thinking about the degrees and angles, just follow the drawing on the sign!

Rally Caution

When you are training for left turns of any type, it can help to put your lead behind your legs. Do *not* do that in a competition, however!

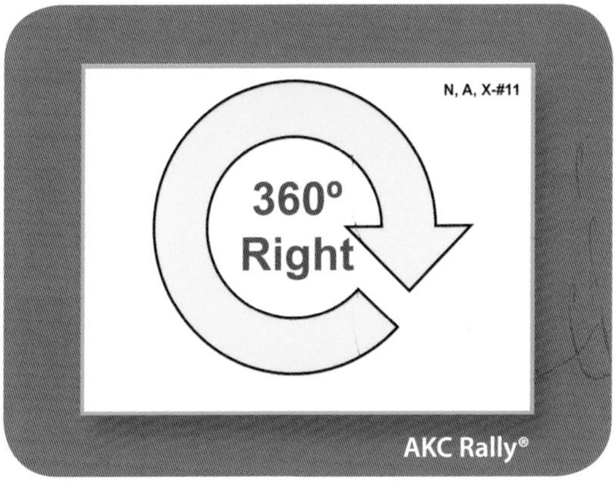

360-Degree Right Turn or 360-Degree Right (Turn)

This time, you will turn to the right and continue in a complete circle. You will end up heading in the exact same direction you were going—just a little dizzy perhaps! You may have heard this exercise described as "circle right" in obedience class. Because you are turning to the right, your dog will have to move briskly to keep up with you. He is on the "outside" of the circle. You do not have to do a tight pivot, but you don't want to do a huge circle either. This is another turn in which your left shoulder cue—moving it forward just a little bit—can be very helpful to your dog.

Many dogs like this sign and enjoy doing fast spins around you. Just make sure that you go far enough that you have done a complete circle and that you are still going in the same direction. Check sign numbers if you need to!

Kate's shoulder and hand (finger) cues, as well as her footwork, alert Queezle to a right 270- or 360-degree turn coming up.

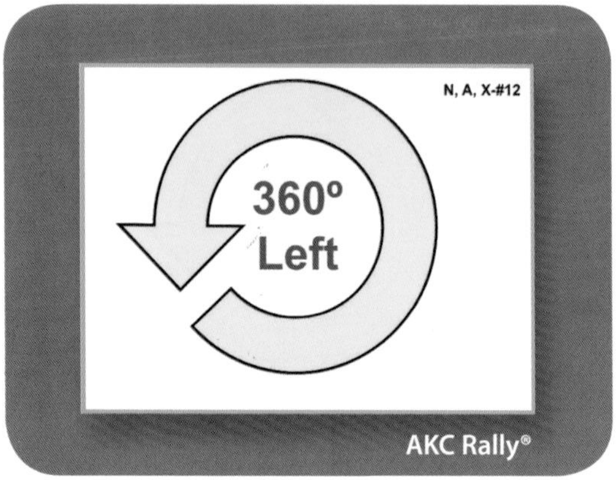

360-Degree Left Turn or 360-Degree Left (Turn)

Now you get to do another complete circle but this time turning to the left. This will put your dog on the "inside" of the circle, so he will need to slow way down or even just stand and pivot. Use your left shoulder cue, tipping it back a bit to warn him he needs to slow down or greatly shorten his stride.

Turn all the way around, doing a complete circle, and you should end up heading in the same direction you were going. Check the sign numbers if you aren't sure.

This sign tends to be a bit harder for most dogs than the right circle. At first, your dog may tend to bump into your leg if he misses the cue that you are turning. Try to warn him with the use of his name or an attention word. This is an excellent exercise to train and practice with your leash behind your legs!

Kate uses both a hand (finger) cue and her shoulder cue to tell Queezle that this will be a 270- or 360-degree left turn.

The last Novice turn sign is a tricky one for most handlers, although the dogs seem to catch on right away. This is a Level 2 sign in the APDT.

Left About Turn

You and your dog move forward as a team. Now, do an about turn to your left so that you turn to the left and end up heading in the opposite direction from the way you were traveling. While you go to the left, your dog will go to the right and do an about turn. So your dog moves behind and around you. You should end up with the dog back in *heel* position, both of you facing in the same direction, and it should be the opposite direction from your approach to this sign. You then move on briskly to the next sign.

This is one of those signs that your body needs to figure out. Your muscle memory will then do the sign easily and correctly without your brain interfering. As you turn to the left, switch your leash to your right hand. You can incorporate a hand signal into this move to help your dog understand where he is to go. Using an *around* command or your right *finish* command may also help. As you both turn, move your leash back to your left hand.

You may want to practice this sign without a dog at first. Dogs seem to catch on to this sign quickly and find it rather fun. Handlers seem to feel very confused and perhaps a bit klutzy at first, but once you get this turn down, it is fun and smooth.

CAMP JACKPOT
STAFF

Basic Rally Exercises: Moving

8

Every rally course is tied together with the moving exercises. These exercises can be simple and straightforward, like the Changes of Pace, or they can be complex maneuvers, like the Side Step Right. All of them will require you and your dog to move right along (although not as briskly for the Slow Pace!) and to work as a team, always with your dog in the *heel* position. Having good attention is essential while moving. Moving exercise signs will be on your right, with the exception of the Side Step Right.

Slow Pace

For the Slow Pace, both you and your dog should show a definite change of speed. The change of pace should be obvious to anyone watching, as well as to the judge. To slow down, help your dog with a shoulder cue as well as a verbal cue. For the shoulder cue, tilt your shoulders back just a touch. This body language will warn your dog to slow down. Verbally, try to use a stretched-out, easy word like "Slooooow." Many dogs will respond to the cadence of your voice.

Ideally, you will start your change of pace at the sign. This sign will be on your right. Continue at the slow pace until a sign orders you to change—either to a normal pace or to the Finish. At the Novice or Level 1 trials, if the Slow is used, it is generally a fairly short sequence.

Kate's shoulder is back, cueing Queezle for a Slow Pace.

Rally Caution

When a change of pace is included in the course, be sure that you do actually speed up or slow down. Do this by changing your stride length or your pace. Your dog must clearly move more slowly or more quickly. The change must be obvious to the judge.
So remember to practice some long sets of Slow Pace heeling. Use your attention words, and encourage your dog to focus on you.

When you get up into the Advanced levels, the judge may use a long Slow to help separate out her top dogs. Many dogs will tend to lag, swing wide, or forge when they get impatient with the slow pace.

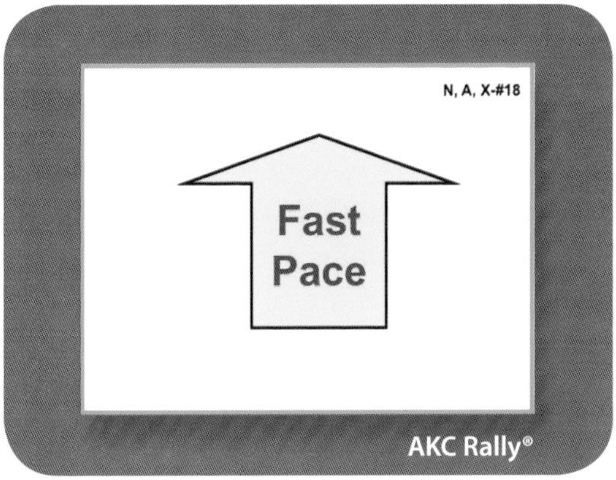

Fast Pace

The Fast Pace sign is one that most dogs love, but it can be tricky to perform well. Both you and your dog must show an obvious change of pace—this time speeding up. Again, the change should be obvious to anyone watching and to the judge. This does not mean a full-out run. A brisk jog will work for most dogs and handlers.

The hard part about this sign is that dogs often feel as if they have been released from the pressure of concentrating on their work. You want that increased speed, but you also want your dog to stay in *heel* position.

To get increased speed, use those shoulders once again. A slight tilt forward will signal your dog that you are going to move faster. You may choose to add a verbal cue. If so, make it short and forceful. "Let's go," "Quick," or "Hustle" are commonly used commands.

The handler is using her body to cue her Sheltie to move faster.

Some dogs will tend to bounce and leap while doing the Fast Pace. As long as they stay in approximate *heel* position, this should be okay. Try to encourage your dog to simply lengthen his stride or canter instead of bounce, but don't blow his enthusiasm. Dogs who lag will be very obvious on the Fast Pace. For those dogs, your goal is to make this move fun. In training, as you speed up, throw a toy or treat, like a Nylabone, ahead of you and let him race to it.

For the dog who wants to race ahead, possibly even turning in front of you, the lead behind your legs is a good training tool.

Normal Pace

This sign will follow the signs above. So your course will have Slow Pace, then Normal Pace or Fast Pace, and then Normal Pace. Returning to Normal Pace requires different cues for each pace changes. If you are on a Slow Pace, as you approach the Normal Pace sign you will need to shift your shoulder forward a bit. A slight lean is fine, but don't be too obvious. You may want to use one of your verbal cues to encourage your dog to rev back up to his regular speed.

Coming off Fast Pace will require the opposite. You now need to lean back a bit and straighten your body. Use a long, easy verbal command. The Normal Pace sign will appear on your righthand side. You should be back at the regular speed right at or close to the sign. Again, your regular pace should be an obvious speed change from the Slow or the Fast.

Rally Profile

Margo With Raisin, Charlie, and Cooper

Margo started with rally back in 2003, with her dog 4-H club, the Chow Hounds. She was working her lovely Standard Poodle, Raisin, in obedience and felt that rally would be a fun sport for both of them. Raisin was a rescue dog—and finally getting things right in her fourth home! They competed in the APDT first and then moved on to the AKC.

Margo finds rally to be a great sport for all three of her dogs. "What I like most about rally is that you get the chance to talk to your dog throughout the exercises. It is a nice boost of encouragement for your dog." Her dogs enjoy the fact that each rally course is different, so they constantly get to try out new things.

Margo's current dogs are Charlie, a German Shorthaired Pointer, and Cooper, a Border Terrier. They love getting to perform jumps in the Advanced levels in rally, and teaching the Over was quite simple. The Moving Down has been the trickiest sign. Both dogs like to pretend that they are all the way down. Still, that is Margo's favorite sign—maybe because of the challenge.

Indoor trials are the way to go for Margo. She prefers not having to worry about rain, mud, and wind. She also likes courses with lots of about turns and tricky turns so that her dogs have to pay attention and focus on her.

Margo stresses the importance of the walk-throughs when you are trialing. "You learn so much when doing your walk-through. The best part is that you can ask the judge any last-minute questions you have about a sign or two."

Why try rally? "It's a really fun sport to try. You and your dog work as a team. It is not like obedience, where you do the same pattern over and over. Rally switches things up, and your dog is more willing to work and listen." Margo has gone on to do formal obedience as well and feels that rally was good preparation for her dogs.

"I think rally is a *great* way to learn how to train a dog. Dogs are willing to work and eager to please you because of the verbal encouragement." Certainly, rally has paid off for Margo and her dogs!

Moving Side Step Right

This is a "hybrid" sign. It is a moving exercise, but it also incorporates a slight change of direction. Think of it as changing lanes on a highway. The sign will be directly in front of you, just like a turn sign on an AKC course and most APDT courses. You and your dog move forward at a brisk pace. Take a step to the right, leading off with your right foot. Then continue in a straight line. Ideally, your dog will smoothly move right with you. The sign will end up being passed on your left side. Make sure that you leave room for your dog!

In the APDT, if the direction change is to be performed after the sign, you will do the same movement but after you have passed the sign. Be sure to ask the judge on an APDT course where she wants this sign

Kate uses her body and her hand to cue Queezle for the sideways step.

performed. The actual flow of the course may make it clear, but ask during your briefing if the judge doesn't mention it herself.

We now come to some of the really fun signs. The Spirals and Weaves appeal to most dogs because they don't have to stop and sit or break their forward movement. They catch on to bending and spinning quickly and don't seem to get dizzy like many of us do. There are certain challenges for the handler, however, such as making sure that neither you nor your dog wipe out the cones used to mark these exercises. For the Spirals, you also need to keep track of exactly where you are in the exercise.

Spiral Right—Dog Outside

This sign is the same for courses in both the APDT and the AKC. As you approach this station, you will see three cones. The sign itself may be next to the first cone or off to the side.

The cones are in a straight line, with about 6 to 8 feet (2 to 2.5 m) of space between them in the AKC. In the APDT, they may be as close together as 5 feet (1.5 m). That can be tight for big dogs like Newfoundlands!

Walk along the cones with the dog on the outside, and turn to the right at the end of the cones. Then walk back to the first cone, turn right again, but this time only walk as far as the second cone. Turn there and return to the start. Now turn again but this time only go around the first cone. How far you loop around that first cone will depend on where your next sign is. It is important that when you walk the course you figure out where you will need to exit the Spiral. If you draw out your path, it will look like a paper clip.

This handler and Corgi are moving around the cone on the outside.

Key things to remember is that you always return to the first cone and that you do not weave between the cones! If you find that you get confused or dizzy when doing Spirals, I suggest that you talk out loud to yourself as you go and count so that you know how many cones you passed the last time. Don't worry about anyone questioning you talking to yourself—you can always say that you were talking to your dog! The sound of your voice will help keep your dog focused on you as well.

Because the dog is on the outside when you do righthand turns, he will have to hustle a bit throughout this station. When training, use your shoulder cue to lean forward a bit and encourage him on, plus throw toys or treats around turns. It may help to work on the Spiral in bits and pieces, doing just the end cones at first, then adding the two-cone stage, etc. At least there are no *sits*!

Spiral Left—Dog Inside

This sign is the reverse of the previous one. You will have the same three cones and do the same pattern, but this time all of your turns will be to the left, putting your dog on the inside. You will go out to the third cone, turn left, and return to the first cone. Then off again but only as far as the second cone this time. Return to the first cone, and loop around it as far as you need to in order to have a smooth flow to your next sign.

There are some things you need to think about with your dog on the inside. Make sure that you leave space for him between you and the cone. If you wrap too tightly, he will end up knocking cones over. Knocking cones down is penalized. Your dog will have to slow down or even back up on the turns because he is on the inside. Use your left shoulder tilted back a touch to cue him to slow down. Big dogs may have to back up a step to make the turns. Once again, if you draw out the pattern, it will look like a paperclip.

It is a good idea to practice the Spirals a few times without your dog so that you master your footwork and path before you add in teaching your dog. Also, these are good exercises to break down into small pieces before you put it all together.

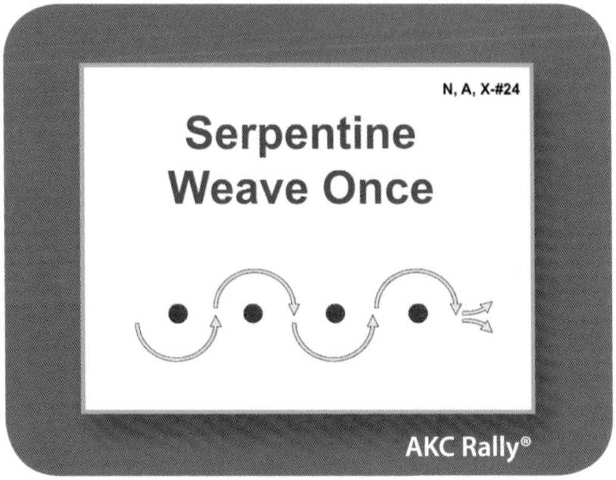

Serpentine Weave Once

This is a sign that dogs seem to love. Anyone who has done agility will recognize the weaving pattern. Four cones are laid out in a straight line, with each cone about 6 feet (2 m) apart. The sign itself is often on the first cone.

Just as in agility, you enter "the weaves" with your dog's left shoulder by the first cone. Because you will be weaving with him, your left shoulder is by the first cone as well. You then weave through the cones as a team and end by passing the last cone. Done correctly, this should place you smoothly in line for the next station.

This station should be done briskly, with you and your dog moving right along. Make sure that you leave room for your dog to pass between you and the cone when you weave to the left. Knocking cones down is penalized. As you weave back to the right, you may have to encourage your dog to speed up a bit. This is another good spot to use your shoulder cues—moving that left shoulder back and forward will help tell your dog to slow down or hurry up. There are no *sits*.

Ann helps Scotty around the cone by holding her shoulder back and with her footwork.

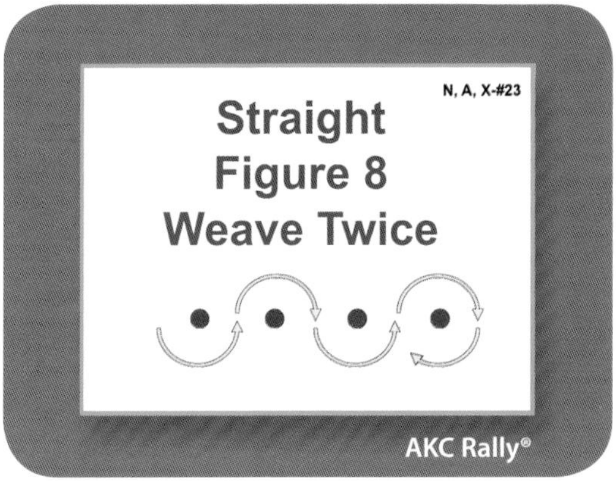

Straight Figure 8 Weave Twice or Straight Figure 8

For this station, you again encounter four cones in a straight line. In AKC courses, the cones are 6 to 8 feet (2 to 2.5 m) apart; in APDT courses, they are about 5 feet (1.5 m) apart.

Just as in agility weaves, you enter with the first cone to the left of you and your dog. This is a team exercise, so both of you will weave together. This time, when you reach the last cone, you turn around it and weave back to the start. Whether or not you need to turn tightly around the last cone at the end will depend on which way the course flows after this exercise. You may simply move out of the last weave, or you may need to turn around that last cone.

Shoulder cues are a big help here, indicating the turns to your dog and helping him adjust his speed—speeding up when he is on the outside and slowing down when he is on the inside.

Rally Speak

When a Weave sign appears in rally, you enter it just as you do in agility. The difference here is that *you* weave as well as your dog!

Advanced-Level Rally Exercises

A number of changes occur when you move on to advanced levels in rally. The biggest change, of course, is that you no longer have a lead on your dog. While you enter the ring on lead, once you are in the ring, the judge will tell you to remove the lead and hand it to the steward. The judge will have you move to the Start sign if you aren't already there.

Before you panic over the loss of your umbilical cord, remember that you still have some big connections to your dog. You have your relationship from training—built on a partnership of trust and teamwork. You also have your voice and hand signals. You can chatter encouragement and in some venues (although not on APDT courses) you can still lure your dog if need be.

The "Advanced" level—terminology used by the AKC—also refers to those types of exercises found in Level 2 of the APDT unless otherwise noted.

Halt, About Turn and Forward or Halt—From Sit—About Turn and Forward

This sign is a change of direction because you will end up heading right back where you came from. The sign is placed directly in front of you, and you move up to it with your dog in *heel* position. You halt and your dog sits. Now, turn to face the opposite direction, with your dog up and moving with you.

Then briskly head off, without letting your dog sit again. The key points here are to stop and have your dog sit. Then turn to your right, with your dog getting up and moving with you. You do not have to do a tight pivot, but you don't want to loop very widely either. Remember, because this sign is a change of direction, the sign will be placed directly in front of you.

You can give your dog a verbal or hand signal to sit, and you may want to give an *attention* command or do something else to alert your dog when you are ready to move. Your dog will be on the outside of the turn, so he will have to

Rally Speak

"Off leash" *only* applies to trials and when in the ring competing. Do not hesitate to train new signs on lead and to practice on lead. Then, remove the lead for short periods to try the exercises without the help of a leash.

hustle to get up from his *sit* and quickly move around you without any lagging. Use your shoulder cue here as well—a slight movement forward with that left shoulder lets your dog know that you are going to turn. You do not want to run over the sign when you turn, so make sure that you have allowed plenty of room for your dog to fit between you and the sign.

If your dog tends to be slow moving, when you are training, you may want to toss a treat or a toy ahead of you as you turn to encourage him to rush around you for it. There is no *sit* after the turn, so you can move off briskly.

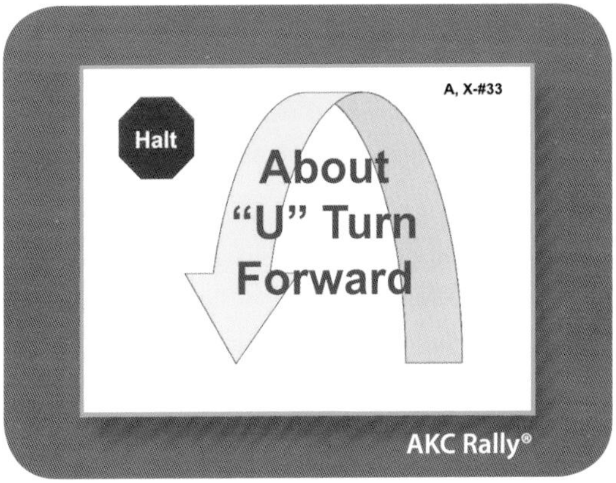

Halt, About "U" Turn and Forward or Halt—From Sit—About "U" Turn and Forward

This is the left-side version of the previous exercise. The sign will be directly in front of you. Heel forward with your dog. You stop, he sits. As a team, turn to your left 180 degrees. As soon as you are facing in the opposite direction, move off briskly. Do not let your dog sit in the *heel* position after the turn. He will be on the inside of the turn, so he must slow way down or even back up a step as you turn. These turns can be cued with your shoulder.

For the Left or "U" About Turn, tip your left shoulder back a touch. This, along with a verbal "Back" or "Get back," signals your dog for the tight left turn. This turn is not meant to be a pivot but should not loop very widely. Bigger dogs will need more room to turn just due to their body size. This exercise can be trained and practiced with a leash behind your legs.

The next sign is a lot of fun for dogs but can give handlers gray hairs due to the control needed. On Advanced or Level 2 courses, your dog will get to do one jump. In AKC competition, the jump could be a single bar jump, a solid panel jump, or a broad jump with the boards laid out as a spread. In the APDT, only bar and panel jumps are used. The basic techniques are the same for all jumps.

The panel jump consists of two standards on either end plus solid panels in between, which is what the dog jumps. The entire thing is white in color. The bar jump has the two standards but only a single bar across between them. The bar is painted in black and white stripes. The broad jump consists of boards of graduated height that lie on the ground. The APDT does not use the broad jump.

The height of the jump will depend on the height of your dog. Dog height is measured at the withers—the area right above their shoulder.

For AKC competition, jump heights are:

- Dogs less than 10 inches (25.5 cm) tall at the withers jump 4 inches (10 cm).
- Dogs 10 inches (25.5 cm) to less than 15 inches (38 cm) tall at the withers jump 8 inches (20.5 cm).
- Dogs 15 (38 cm) inches to less than 20 inches (51 cm) tall at the withers jump 12 inches (30.5 cm).
- Dogs 20 inches (51 cm) and up at the withers jump 16 inches (40.5 cm).
- If the broad jump is used, the height is doubled—remember, this is lying down, though. For dogs jumping 8 inches (20.5 cm), one broad jump board is used; for 16- and 24-inch (40.5- and 61-cm) jump sizes, two boards are used; and three boards are used for dogs jumping 32 inches (81 cm).

In APDT competition, jump heights are:

- Dogs less than 12 inches (30.5 cm) at the withers jump 4 inches (10 cm).
- Dogs 12 inches (30.5 cm) to less than 16 inches (40.5 cm) at the withers jump 8 inches (20.5 cm).
- Dogs 16 inches (40.5 cm) to less than 20 inches (51 cm) at the withers jump 12 inches (30.5 cm).
- Dogs 20 (51 cm) inches or more at the withers jump 16 inches (40.5 cm).
- In the APDT, judges may make allowances for a lower jump height for an older dog or a dog with a disability. In some cases, the jump may be excused entirely.

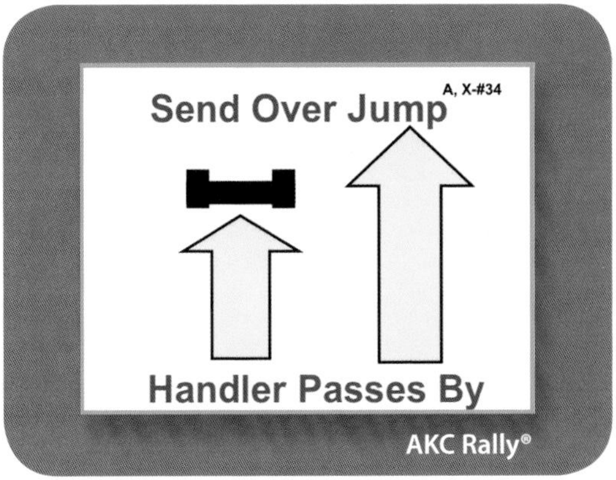

Send Over Jump—Handler Passes By or Send Over Jumps—Handler Runs By

For the AKC, you and your dog heel toward the jump. Tell him to take the jump while you pass by it. You should not stop, pause, or hesitate while sending the dog over the jump, but you are no longer required to run. You must continue moving toward the other side of the jump. Once your dog has gone over the jump and landed, you and your dog, as a team, meet up again, with your dog resuming the *heel* position. Your dog can be called to heel or given a hand signal. He must get back to the *heel* position so that you, as a team, can continue on together. The quicker you are back together, the better. If your dog is much faster than you or tends to jump big, he will probably land ahead of you and need to be called back.

In the APDT, the exercise is more complicated. A line may be marked on the course about 6 feet (2 m) to the right side of the jump. Even without the line, for full credit, you must stay about 6 feet (2 m) to the side of the jump as your dog jumps. This means that you must be over to the side position before your dog actually jumps, and you must stay over until he lands from the jump. Your dog then returns to *heel* position so that you both, as a team, can move on.

Your dog should not return to *heel* and sit in either the AKC or APDT. Instead, as soon as your dog returns to the *heel* position, continue on to the next sign together.

If your dog has never jumped before, start with a very low jump, even just a bar on the floor. Once he learns to go over that, gradually raise the bar up to the required jump height. Never jump your dog on poor footing! His safety is of paramount importance.

For dogs who show reluctance to jump or even step over a bar, you may need some assistance. A friend or family member can stand on the far side of the jump with a treat, or you can have her hold your dog by the collar while you go to the other side. If your dog has a good *stay*, tell him to stay and go over yourself, or have him stay and place a toy or treat on the other side. Most dogs enjoy jumping.

This Bernese Mountain Dog shows good form over the jump.

A dog who truly resists jumping may have a physical problem. The rally jump heights are quite low, but for an overweight, arthritic, or dysplastic dog, even these jumps may be too much. Your rally instructor may pick up on unsound movement or structure and recommend a veterinary exam. Your veterinarian can tell you if it is safe and comfortable for your dog to jump.

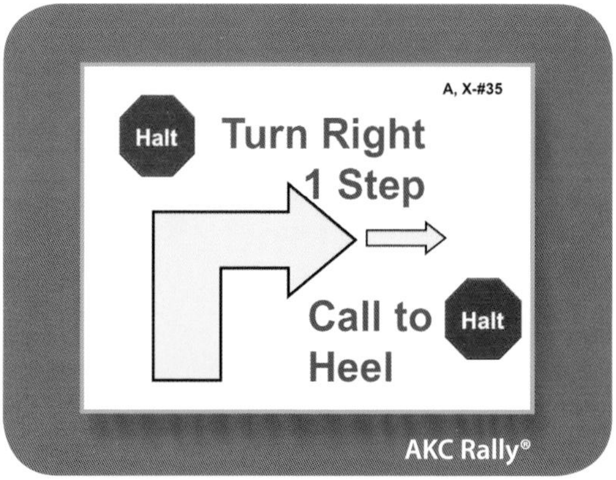

Halt, Turn Right One Step, Call to Heel

This is an AKC sign. To perform this exercise, you and your dog heel up to the sign; it will be in front of you because this is a change of direction. As you stop, your dog should sit in the *heel* position. Tell him to stay. Remember, you can use a verbal command, a hand signal, or both. Then, turn to your right and take one step away from your dog. If you have a big dog, try to take a good-sized step. Once you are stopped, call him up to the *heel* position. Your dog will move up to the *heel* position and sit.

Once your dog is sitting, move on together to the next sign. Big dogs and older dogs who have "limited *sits* per day" seem to question your sanity over this move. It is an excellent way to tighten up heeling and work on correct *heel* position, but if your dog really does not like sitting, try to mix this up in practice with plenty of moving exercises.

Rally Caution

If you do both APDT and AKC Rally®, you will find that, on Advanced and Level 2 courses, some signs are not quite the same between the two venues. Make sure that you are clear in your mind when you walk a course as to which venue and exercise you are looking at.

Halt, Stand Dog, Walk Around

This sign is an introduction to the Novice obedience Stand for Exam. You and your dog move along briskly. When you come to this sign, halt and have your dog sit in *heel* position. Once he is sitting, give the verbal command to stand, use a hand signal, or both. If you need to, you may move a step or so forward in front of your dog to help him stand. You may also touch your dog to position his legs—as in the show ring—or even just to balance out his *stand*.

Once your dog is standing comfortably, take your hands off him and give a *stay* command. This can be verbal, a hand signal, or both. Then, walk around your dog, going counterclockwise, and return to *heel* position. You may repeat the *stay* command as needed.

Kate gives Queezle a *stay* signal as she starts to walk around her.

When you get back to the *heel* position, pause. Take a deep breath and then go on. Taking the breath reminds you of the pause, plus you are generally nervous in a trial, and taking a breath is a good way to calm down!

The signs that require pivots are similar in both the AKC and APDT. In the AKC, these signs come up at the Advanced level. In the APDT, the pivots show up first in Level 1. Pivots are excellent for tightening up the *heel* position and for practicing for the day you get to Utility and need to do the Directed Retrieve exercise with gloves. Some dogs think that pivots are fun, while other dogs wonder why you keep spinning around in a small space and expecting them to move with you. For those dogs, keep the rewards high and emphasize motivation and attitude.

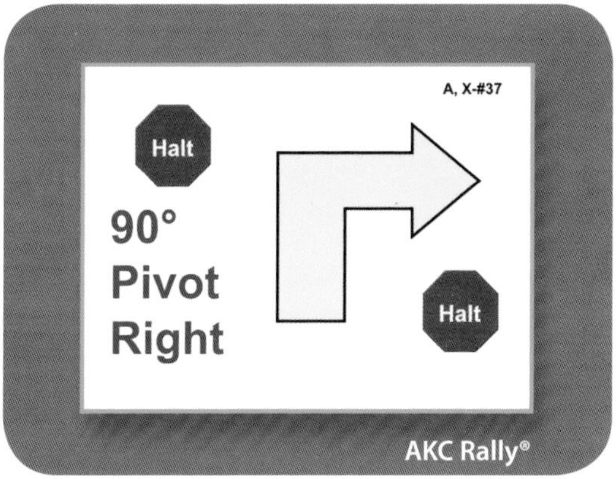

Halt, 90-Degree Pivot Right, Halt

Because the pivot will change your direction, this sign will appear in front of you. As you approach the sign, halt and have your dog sit in the *heel* position. As you pivot 90 degrees to the right, your dog will move with you. Stop with your dog as you face the new direction, and have him sit again. Your dog is on the outside for this pivot, so he will need to get up and move quickly to stay in his correct position. Reward that quick start on his part!

I think of pivots as the "3 Ps." To correctly pivot, *plant* your feet, keeping them on a *pie plate*, and remember your *partner* because you move together. The "plant" reminds me that I am not taking a step. The "pie plate" reminds me to

Rally Profile

Donna and Click

Donna started with AKC Rally® in 2004 and attended the famous midnight trial series in Rochester, New York, to title the first weekend out. Having a young Australian Shepherd, Click, was the perfect excuse to try out a new dog sport.

For Donna, rally is a great sport for a young dog because you can talk to the dog. Click enjoys rally because it is fast paced, so his mind is kept busy. He also loves the jumps at the upper levels.

Donna says that her favorite sign is Start because they can jump right in and go. With an active dog, that is clearly a plus to rally. The Honor can be trying because Click isn't thrilled about staying still. "It is the luck of the draw with the honor," explains Donna. "It could be very short or very long, depending on the dog you have to honor for." She also says "Rally is an excellent venue for a new dog or an inexperienced handler. Rally is less stressful than formal obedience and fun to train." For Donna and Click, rally also helped provide a solid foundation for obedience heeling because many of the rally exercises are like obedience "doodling." Plus, you can retry signs if you make a mistake and "fix" a problem right then and there, all while encouraging your dog. "Rally helped me get my confidence back to get back into obedience," explains Donna. Obviously it worked, as she has now titled two dogs—her Greyhound has an RE title and Click has an RAE 2.

To start the right pivot, Kate uses a treat to lure Queezle.

keep my feet under me and stay basically in the same spot. Finally, the "partner" reminds me that my dog is supposed to move with me.

The pivot exercises are good ones for you to practice without your dog at first. These exercises can be very boring to your dog, so you want to have your part perfected before you train him. Definitely train the pivots on lead first before you try going off lead. That way, your dog will be trained to a fairly precise, tight turn right from the start.

Kate starts moving her feet, staying on her imaginary pie plate.

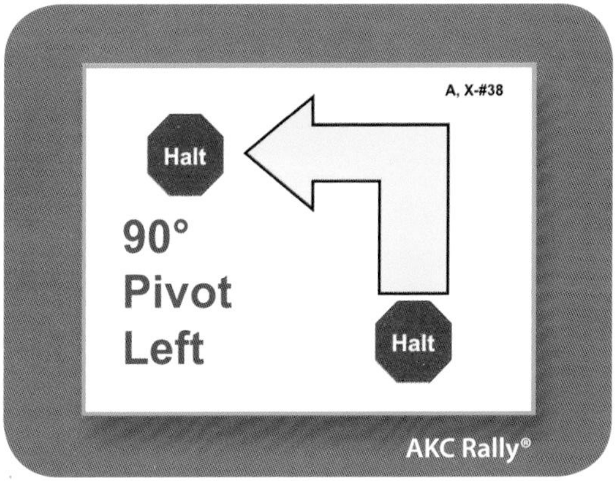

Halt, 90-Degree Pivot Left, Halt

This is the mirror image of the previous sign. Once again, you directly approach the sign and halt. Once your dog is sitting, move as a team to the left in a 90-degree turn. Remember the "3Ps"! No big step here, just spin on your heel. Because you are turning to the left, your dog will be on the inside. He may barely stand before he has to sit again. A big dog may even need to back up a step to stay in position.

This is an excellent time to train with the leash behind your legs. Your dog will learn to stand and pivot on his front legs, letting his back legs move into position.

Again, for a big dog or a dog who is reluctant to sit, these pivots make no sense at all. Why sit when you just have to move a teeny bit and then sit again? You need to be sure that you reward these exercises highly and break up training them with play and fun moving exercises.

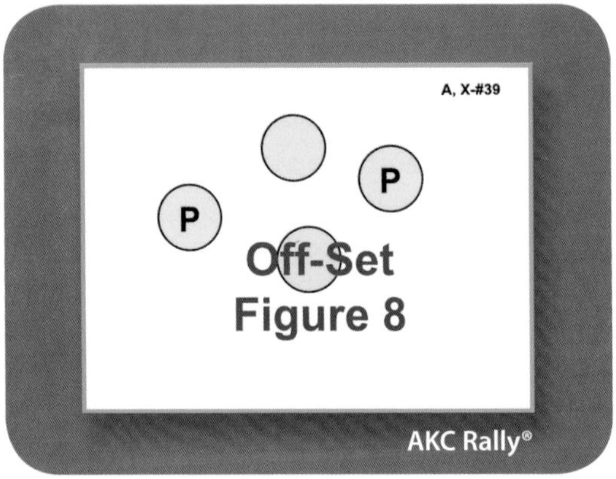

Off-Set Figure 8

This sign and exercise appear in both the Advanced AKC and Level 2 APDT but with some small differences. This station is an introduction to the Figure 8 exercise in obedience heeling but with some added twists. For the AKC, two cones are placed 8 to 10 feet (2.5 to 3 m) apart. These are the "posts" you will heel around for the Figure 8. Cross the center three times to complete the exercise. No *sits* are required. The sign may be to the side or it may be placed right beside the cone where you enter into the Figure 8. Exactly where you enter will be determined by the flow of the course. The path you enter on will lead you to a certain exit, and you want to exit along the course flow.

So far, so good. Encourage your dog on the turns when he is on the outside and keep him back a touch when he is on the inside. Remember to leave room for him to fit between you and the cone. This is an excellent place to use your shoulder cues to speed him up or slow him down.

Things are not quite that simple, however! About 5 to 6 feet (1.5 to 2 m) apart, across the middle of the Figure 8, are two sets of distractions. These can be metal bowls filled with treats and covered with a tight-fitting wire lid—so that

With Queezle in a *sit*, Kate puts the leash behind her and starts to lure her to the left.

Queezle is moving with Kate, tightly by her side.

Now that Queezle is straight, Kate just needs to remind her to sit.

your dog can smell them but hopefully won't manage to snag any!—or they can be toys, either in a container or on the floor. For the APDT, four bowls with metal screens are used—two of them 10 feet (3 m) apart for you to heel your Figure 8 around and two of them 5 feet (1.5 m) apart as added distractions near the middle. All of these bowls contain treats.

You are allowed to give your dog verbal reminders to heel with you, pay attention to you, and to leave the distractions—and you may need all three! Your dog is off lead, so you can't count on a lead correction to keep him from rewarding himself with a nice treat or toy. Definitely train and practice this exercise on lead, however.

A further note of caution: When the Off-Set Figure 8 is included in a course, your dog may smell the treats or notice the toys even while doing other exercises. You must be aware of these distractions at all times.

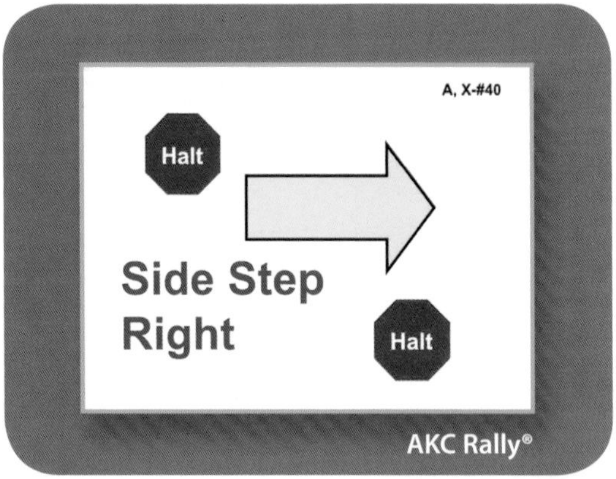

Halt, Side Step Right, Halt

This is a sign that can be easily confused with the Halt, Turn Right One Step, Call to Heel. Make sure that you know which is which when you walk the course!

For this exercise, you and your dog walk briskly up to the sign, which should appear in front of you. You will come to a halt, and your dog should sit by your side. Then, take a step to the right, cueing your dog to move with you as you move. Stop after the single step and have your dog also stop and sit again. Ideally, he will follow right next to your left leg as you take the step. It is important to give your dog a cue or warning that he is to come with you. You can give a verbal command, encourage him, and pat your leg if need be.

When you finish, proceed forward, this time with the sign on your left.

Kate uses the leash behind her leg to help Queezle with the Side Step Right.

We now come to a series of Recall signs with fronts and finishes or forwards. These must be distinguished from the Novice signs that also involve fronts and finishes. Make sure that you study the signs, and look at them carefully when you walk a course. You don't want to be the one responsible for a big ten-point error!

Halt, Call Dog Front, Finish Right

For this exercise, you and your dog approach with the sign off to your right. Come to a halt and have your dog sit by your side in the *heel* position. Now comes the tricky part. *Without* moving your feet, call your dog to come sit in front. For a big dog, you may want to teach a *go* command to get him up and moving forward, and then you can call him back to the front position. Small dogs can generally simply get up and swing over. For most dogs, you can help by initially guiding or luring them forward and then around in a tight turn to sit in front. Some dogs respond very well to a release word after they sit at your side, which gets them up so that you guide them into the front position.

Once your dog is sitting in front, give the command—verbal, hand signal, or both—to finish by going around you to the right. He should then sit in the *heel* position. After the dog sits, you can proceed.

Once again, a lot of *sits* are worked into one station. Make sure that you reward this exercise well and mix in plenty of moving exercises and play.

Halt, Call Dog Front, Finish Left

This sign is the left version of the previous. Do the same approach and come to a halt with your dog sitting in the *heel* position. Again, without moving your feet at all, encourage him to get up and swing around so that he comes to sit in front. Once he is sitting in front, give your command for the finish to the left. Remember, no moving your feet for this either! As your dog comes around and gets into the *heel* position, use a *sit* command if you need to. After he sits, proceed together as a team.

Because you mastered 90-degree pivots earlier, you can now move on to two additional pivots. These signs will appear in front of you, as the exercises will change your direction.

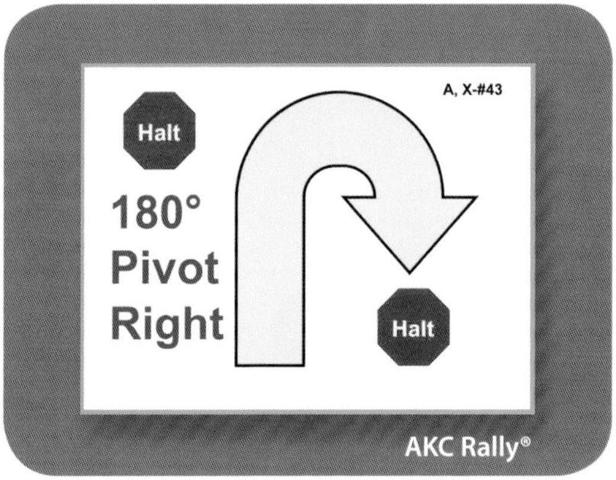

Halt, 180-Degree Pivot Right, Halt

This pivot is a bit more extensive than the 90-degree ones you have already mastered. You and your dog will approach the sign as a team and halt, with your dog sitting in the *heel* position. Now, turn around so that you are facing the other way but still keeping the "3 Ps" of pivots in mind: Plant your feet, keep them on a pie plate, and partner so that you move together. Because this is a pivot to the right, spin around to the right until you are facing opposite the direction you were heading. Ideally, your dog will move right with you.

With a pivot to the right, your dog will be on the outside of the turn. He will have to hustle a bit to stay in the correct position. This is another place to use your shoulder cues. Move that left shoulder a bit forward to cue your dog to move ahead quickly. Once you have completed your turn, stop; Your dog should sit by your side.

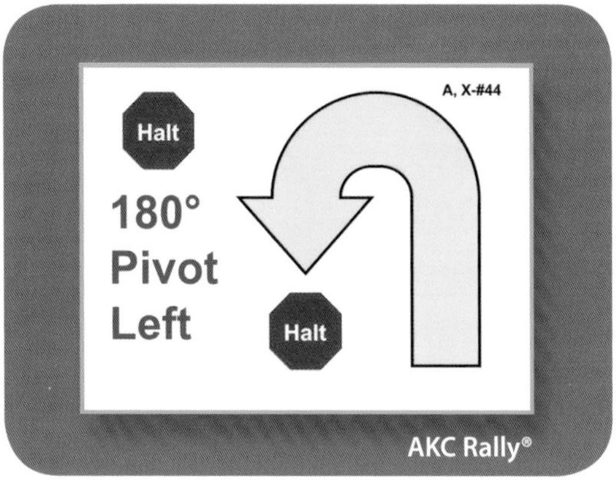

Halt, 180-Degree Pivot Left, Halt

You are now doing the reverse of the previous exercise. Approach the sign, which should be directly in front of you. Stop and have your dog sit by your side. Now pivot 180 degrees to your left so that you end up facing the direction from which you just came. Keep those "3 Ps" in mind! This time your dog will be on the inside of the turn. He will have to turn very tightly or even back up a step or two to remain in position. Use your shoulder cue, turning that left shoulder back a bit to remind him to stay back and go slowly. Once you are facing in the new direction, halt and have your dog sit in the *heel* position.

This is a good exercise to teach with a lead behind your legs to help your dog learn to spin—keeping his front legs still but moving his rear legs around to complete the pivot.

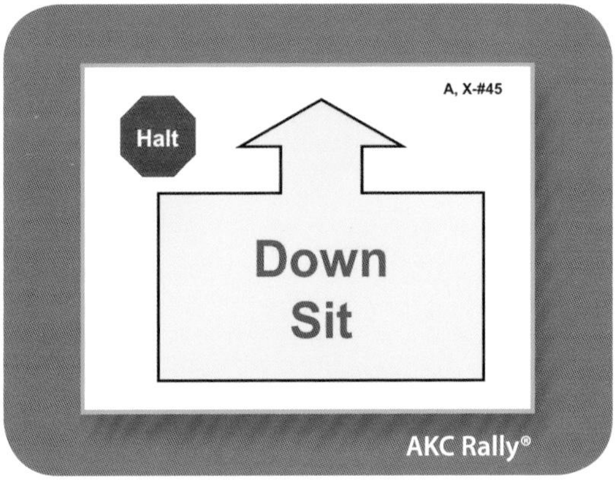

Halt, Down, Sit (AKC) or Halt, Sit, Down, Sit (APDT)

This last AKC Advanced sign is a Level 1 sign in the APDT. The wording is slightly different on the two signs. However, the exercise is performed the same way for both venues. This is a stationary exercise, and the sign will be on your right.

When you reach the sign, halt and have your dog sit at your side. Then tell or signal him to lie down. You are not supposed to move yourself in the AKC, but you can move to help your dog in the APDT. Once your dog is lying down—be sure that his elbows are down too—give him the signal to sit. This can be verbal, a hand signal alone, or both together. Once he is back in a *sit*, proceed to the next exercise.

10 Excellent-Level Rally Exercises

You have now reached the top of the heap in rally competitions. The signs and exercises at Excellent and Level 3 will integrate bits of obedience and plenty of doodling—the little exercises that improve precision. As always, it is important to keep your dog interested and enthused. You may still use plenty of verbal encouragement but no luring. You may not clap your hands or pat your leg to encourage your dog. Footwork may be more exacting. While you had one jump in Advanced or Level 2, you will now have to take two jumps. It may be the same jump but taken in opposite directions, or it could be two entirely different jumps. If you have a *stand* exercise on your course, you are no longer allowed to move to help your dog or to touch him. This is hard to remember at times, but by now you are an experienced rally trainer and competitor.

Your dog will be off lead when performing, but by now your partnership should be quite strong and steady. Even though your dog is now at the Excellent level and you will be competing off lead, you should still train with a lead much of the time. A short, thin lead can easily be put on and off your dog (disappearing into a pocket or around your neck) so that you train both with and without its aid. Leads are especially helpful for learning some of the pivots.

Once your dog has earned the RE title for Rally Excellent in AKC Rally®, you may choose to continue to compete for the RAE title. Dogs competing for this title have already earned their RA and RE. They now enter both Rally Advanced B and Rally Excellent B at trials. To earn this title, the dog must pass both classes on the same day ten times.

The "Excellent" level—terminology used by the AKC—also refers to those types of exercises found in Level 3 of the APDT unless otherwise noted.

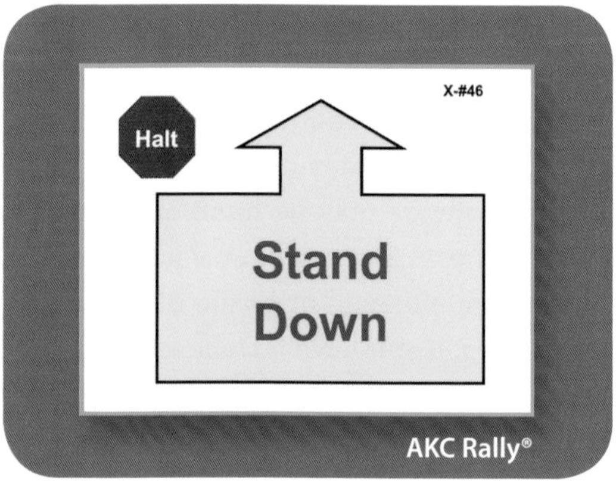

Halt, Stand, Down

This is an AKC sign. Move forward and the sign will be on your right. Halt and have your dog sit in the *heel* position.

The next move is for your dog to stand. Unlike in Novice or Advanced, at the Excellent level, you are not allowed to touch your dog or to move forward. Your feet must remain planted in your halt.

You are allowed to use a verbal command, hand signal, or both. Once your dog is standing, ask him to down. Again, you can use both verbal and hand

Kate and Queezle demonstrate the Halt With *Sit*, which is the first part of this station.

The *stand* is the second step.

And a nice *down* in place finishes the exercise!

signals or just one. When your dog is fully down—even those elbows!—give the command to move forward and go off at a brisk pace. Your dog will need to get up right away from the *down* so that he does not lag behind as you head off.

Often, dogs tend to try to curl around in front of you when they down. While training, use your left foot out in front a bit to prevent this and to keep your dog straight. You may not move that foot in a real trial though.

Many dogs enjoy doing these versions of "puppy push-ups," in which you mix in the *stand*, *down*, and *sit*. Make sure to be upbeat when teaching this, and use rewards liberally.

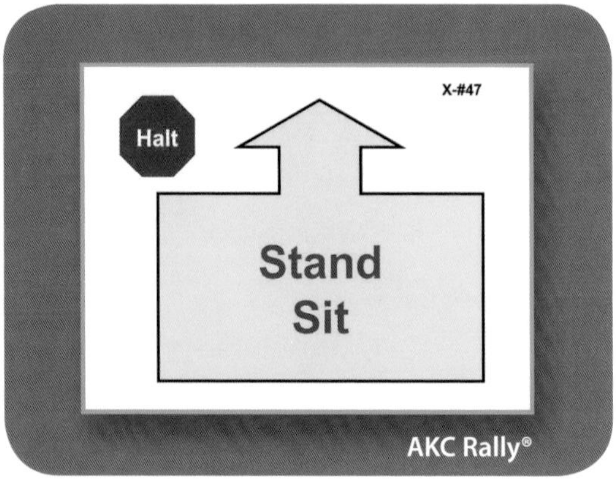

Halt, Stand, Sit

This is another AKC sign and another variation on the puppy push-up. This time, you approach the sign and have your dog sit. From the *sit*, have him stand. As with the previous sign, you are not allowed to touch him or to move forward yourself. You can use verbal and hand signals or both. Once your dog is standing, have him sit. When he is sitting (hopefully in the *heel* position), proceed to the next sign.

These exercises that require your dog to change positions are actually very good for his muscle development. Plus, rally forces trainers to practice finishes and turns to both directions. This keeps our dogs from becoming one-sided, and it helps with even muscle development.

Moving Stand, Walk Around Dog or Moving Stand, Walk Around

This exercise appears in both the AKC Excellent and APDT Level 3. With your dog, approach the sign, which is on your right. As you get close, tell your dog to stand. You can use a verbal cue, a hand signal, or both. Do not pause while doing this, but continue walking in a counterclockwise direction around your dog and return to *heel* position. Once you are back in the *heel* position, pause—remember that deep breath!—then continue.

Kate gives Queezle the signal to stand as she moves to go in front of her.

Kate moves briskly around her as Queezle holds the *stand-stay*.

Kate returns to the *heel* position, takes a deep breath, and smiles at Queezle, who did a nice job.

Your dog should not sit at any time during this exercise. He must go right to the *stand* and remain standing until you move forward together. You may give a *stay* command and/or signal as you walk around him. Remember, basically, your dog is already standing since you have been heeling. What you really need is a *stay*. Some dogs do this exercise best if you simply say "Stay" as you walk around.

An easy way to teach this is to have a treat in your left hand. As you say or signal the *stand*, pop the treat into his mouth. Then remind him to stay as you walk around.

Moving Down, Walk Around Dog

This is an AKC sign. With your dog, approach the sign, which should be on your right. Without stopping or pausing, give him the command to down. This can be a hand signal, a verbal signal, or both. The key here is to have your dog go directly from walking to lying down with no pause or *sit* between the two positions. Your job, meanwhile, is to continue directly on, going counterclockwise around your dog to return to the *heel* position. You can remind him to stay once he is lying down.

When you are back in the *heel* position, take that deep breath again, do your pause, and then move forward, with your dog going directly from his *down* position to moving in *heel* position. He will have to hustle to stay in position.

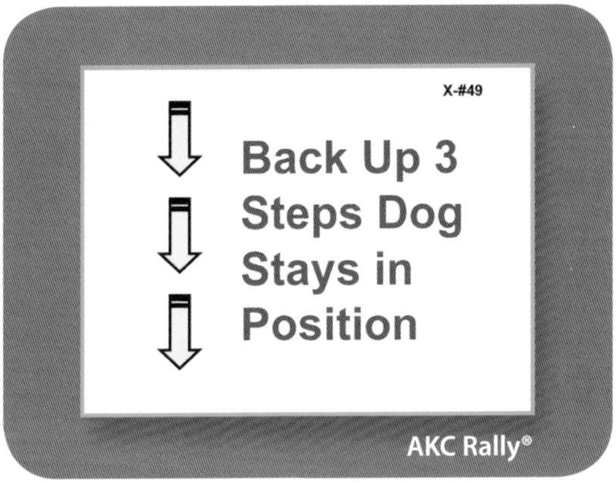

Back Up 3 Steps (Dog Stays in Position) or Moving Back Up (Heel Back 3 Steps Then Forward)

This exercise is a true test of *your* footwork, as well as of your dog's training and agility. Be sure to practice this without your dog so that you are confident in your footwork before you start to train him.

When you reach the sign on your right, back up three steps without coming to a pause first. As soon as you make that third step, resume going forward. Meanwhile, your dog is backing up next to you in the *heel* position. The number of steps he takes does not matter, but *you* must take three steps backward. It may help to count out loud (or quietly to yourself) as you do the three steps.

Rally Caution

Do not confuse the Moving Down, Walk Around Dog with the Stop and Down in AKC Novice or Moving Down and Forward in APDT Level 2. In all three exercises, your dog needs to go from standing or moving directly to a *down.* But for the Novice sign and the APDT sign, you stay in an approximate *heel* position the whole time. In the Moving Down, Walk Around Dog, you must walk around your dog.

Rally Profile

Carol and the Corgis

For Carol, rally came at just the right time. "I was competing with my dog in obedience and hitting a wall concerning heeling and attention. We'd been competing in agility for a few years, and I thought rally would be a good bridge between the two." Her Pembroke Welsh Corgis have competed all the way to the Excellent level, and at her first trial, they won their class of 78 dogs with a perfect score of 100. Rally training worked, as she and Scout became a great team in obedience as well!

Her current competitor, Buck, loves the jumping stations. In fact, Corgis tend to love anything that moves right along. The drawback to rally for a Corgi is that they often have long backs, and so sitting isn't as natural for them as lying down. Rally courses tend to have plenty of *sits*.

For Carol and Buck, backing up is the hardest station to train for—it's that long back again!—and also the Honor. The Spiral is Carol's favorite rally exercise to do with her dogs. "It is all about the footwork and giving your dog enough space to smoothly execute the exercise. We gain a lot of time doing this."

Carol says "Rally is a great sport for everyone to compete in! It is really a way to help ensure that all of your walks are pleasant and that your dog is responsive to you. Find a good class that is fun and promotes positive reinforcement training methods."

Sara has Echo standing in the *heel* position and starts to cue her with her hand to back up.

Echo has to work hard, but she starts to back up.

Again, I suggest that you practice this footwork without your dog first so that you can move confidently. I also find that it helps me to do sort of a "rocking" step for my last step backward. This gets me thinking right away about going forward and not pausing. If you pause, your dog may try to sit. Moving quickly seems to help my dogs as well, but it can unbalance the human partner.

Teaching your dog to back up can be done in a number of ways. For some dogs, simply putting your hand in front of their face and saying "Back" as you move backward will suffice. Most dogs need a bit more help learning to control their feet as they go backward. Dogs tend to move wide, going out from your body and leaving the *heel* position as you back up. To prevent this tendency from becoming a habit, it helps to practice this exercise against a wall or in a narrow hallway. Have your dog next to you, sandwiched between you and the wall. Then, as you give your command and/or signal to back up, he will have to stay straight. It can help to have a treat in your left hand.

This is another good time to use your lead behind your legs. The pressure on the lead, along with your verbal and hand signal, will help your dog understand what you want. Some trainers initially teach "back" by standing in front of their dog, then walking toward the dog, saying "Back." Your dog will move, if for no other reason than to keep from being run over by you! This will help him learn to control his feet. You then need to transition to the side position, however.

Another alternative is to use a lightweight dowel to tap on your dog's chest as you say "Back." Remember—a tap, not a whack! Once your dog starts to move back away from the dowel, pair your command to the action.

Honor

This is an AKC sign and is required for every Excellent class. The whole procedure is a bit different from your normal rally exercise. The honor is not incorporated into the flow of the course. You run your Excellent course, and after you pass the Finish sign, you are given your lead back. For this exercise, you must have a 6-foot (2-m) lead.

Rally Speak

In rally, an *honor* is not something you call the judge. It means that your dog holds his *stay* and does not interfere with the performance of the currently working dog. The term is used in field work as well.

Once your dog is on lead, you proceed to the Honor station. The judge will have designated a *sit* or a *down* as the Honor position. You stay at the Honor sign with your dog in either the *sit* or *down* at the *heel* position as the next team lines up to start its course run. When the judge tells that team "Forward," you tell your dog to stay, then go to the end of your lead and turn to face your dog.

Your dog must remain in the *sit* or *down* and where he was told to stay while the other dog runs his course. A steward will be designated to observe you. Once that dog passes the Finish sign, the steward will tell you "Exercise finished," and you return to your dog and leave the ring. You are not allowed to retry this sign, so if your dog gets up, changes position, or moves, you will lose the full credit for the station.

With a good course design, the Honor station is out of the way of the dog running the course but does allow for some distraction for both dogs. Ideally, you want to practice this station both ways— with your dog running while another dog honors and with your dog as the one who must stay in an Honor position.

This sign will help prepare your dog for the long *sit-stays* and *down-stays* in obedience.

5
Left
Turn
4
3
Send Over Jump
Handler Runs By
2
Halt
Down
Walk Around
Dog
1
360°
Left
START

Putting It All Together: Sequencing

Now that you have mastered the individual exercises, your next step is to start stringing exercises together. The rally course at a trial will consist of a series of exercises, with the exact number and type of exercises depending on venue and level. You will need to move briskly and confidently around the course, following the exercises in correct numerical order and performing the stations as required.

Start Practicing Short Sequences

It is best to start practicing short sequences. This is especially true if your dog is young, old, or simply short on attention. You may want to set up a mini course at home with just three or four signs. That way, you are only asking for attention and precision for a very short period and you can quickly work through the sequences and give your dog a big reward. Having a jackpot of special treats can be a great inducement to a reluctant worker!

Eventually, even dogs with short attention spans will be able to do more and more exercises in a row. Once your dog can do 10 or 12 signs in a row, you are close to being ready to compete. Still, every once in a while, break off and have a big celebration with play, praise, and a toy or treats partway through a practice course. That way, your dog never knows when the reward will come and he will stay "up" and working hard on the exercises.

Make a Mini Course

Make sure that your mini courses have a mix of stationary and moving signs. Also, be sure to include those signs you really don't like. Those tend to be the signs you avoid practicing, even if it is just subconsciously. It is also better for your dog if you mix up the signs so that you don't do four of the Recall signs, for example. Dogs like variety, just as we do. If your dog is one of those who feels that *sits* or *downs* are a lot of work, try not to have too many stationary exercises in a row.

Learn to Judge Your Spacing and Timing

An important part of sequencing is learning to judge your spacing and timing to help your dog. You want to be sure that you give him enough room to maneuver, especially if he is large. On signs such as Back Up Three Steps, plan where to begin backing up so that you don't run into other signs or cones. For 360s, you must have room for the spin. On the Inside Spiral, train yourself to leave room for your dog between you and the cones. For a course with jumps, think about how to control your dog's jump, where he is likely to land, and when to be prepared to call him back to heel.

Keep your dog up and focused, and make sure that you leave room for the cones!

Plan your movements so that you can guide your dog smoothly from one sign to

Rally Speak

When you start to compete in rally you will notice that your confirmation sheet includes a "walk-through" time. This is time set aside for handlers to walk through the course without their dogs. Generally, this is a ten-minute period. For large classes, the walk-through may be divided into several groups.

the next. If you are comfortable with where you are going, your dog will move more confidently as well. You should know the course well enough that you can move right along and hopefully not have to look for numbers. Having said that, most of us do get "lost" once in a while, and luckily, the sequentially numbered stations will help you figure out where to go next!

A good course will flow very naturally and make it easy for you to move along. Think about any transitions, such as changes of pace or turns. For stations such as Weaves, Spirals, and the Off-Set Figure 8, plan where you will want to exit the exercise. Look ahead for the next sign as your guide. If you plan a few steps ahead, you can make your run smoother and make it easier for your dog to stay with you without a tight lead. Again, if you move confidently and smoothly, your dog will come along smoothly as well.

Walk the Course

An important step in starting to sequence is learning to walk the course and make the most of your time allowed to do so. The judge will have set aside a certain amount of time for handlers to walk the course without their dogs. If the class is very large, the walk-through may be split into groups; otherwise, everyone walks together. It can be disconcerting at first to try to concentrate with a bunch of other people walking around too, but you will learn to adjust.

I recommend that you first do a quick walk-through just to follow the numbers and get a feel for the flow of the course. Make sure that you follow the numbers exactly and don't miss any stations! After that first quick walk, go slowly the second time through. Make sure that you read each sign carefully—getting the right finish in your mind on Recall signs, turns correct, planning your exits from the Weaves, Spirals, and Figure 8 if need be, etc. Then, ideally, walk through a third time, this time actually doing the signs as if your dog was with you. Don't worry about looking or feeling silly—everyone else will be doing this too!

Susan is looking ahead to the next sign.

Practice, Practice, Practice

To practice at home, set up mini courses—eventually even full-length ones. Your goal here is to mix up the type of signs, including both stationary and moving signs. Use your turn signs to achieve a relatively smooth flow at first. Later, use diagonals for a trickier flow. If you have a friend to train with, take turns setting up the course. Also, make sure that you use all of the signs at some point. We tend to pick those signs that we and our dogs do well and ignore those exercises that may be difficult.

If you are in a class, your instructor will design courses or have you run courses she has collected while competing. These can be invaluable, as you know that they are realistic. It can also help you decide if there are certain judges you would prefer to enter under. Judges who own large-breed dogs tend to give more space for moving around the ring (although not always).

Rally Caution

Many courses, especially at the higher levels, will have Spirals and Weave exercises that use the same cones. Be very aware of this when you walk the course to plan your flow.

Some judges develop a reputation for fast, smooth-flowing courses, while others are known for tricky, twisty courses. Your instructor can help you here.

Check out resources like the Match Show bulletin for a listing of rally run-throughs, show-n-go's, and matches. The more practice courses you try, the better prepared you will be.

Concentrate as you walk your course.

An important part of course design and learning to sequence is figuring out where to come out of exercises like the Spiral. An extra quarter turn can make the whole course flow much more smoothly. The same holds true for the Off-Set Figure 8 exercise. You can enter in a variety of ways and still qualify, but certain paths are easier for you and your dog.

When planning practice courses at home, try to alternate stationary, moving, and turn signs. Too many *sits* in a row can be discouraging to an older or large dog. After all, getting up and down can be tiring! Some dogs fail to see the point of sitting so often when they realize that they will be getting up and moving again very soon. Be sure to reward *sits* frequently while training.

Once you feel up to the challenge, try running a course "blind." This does not mean with a blindfold! Have someone else set up a course and then run it without a chance to walk through it first. You might want to try this without your dog the first few times so that you don't discourage him with your hesitation or lack of flow. This is a real test of how well you know the signs and exercises! This challenge is offered as a nonregular class at some AKC trials.

Rally Profile

Joan Greenwald

Joan is a well-known competitor and judge in our area, competing with her stunning Landseer Newfoundlands and always judging with patience and a good sense of humor.

Joan first started working in rally in 2003, in the American Kennel Club (AKC) venue. The Newfoundland National Specialty was offering rally, and Joan thought it would be fun to try. Her dog found it was a lot of fun—enough fun that Joan and her dog now have an RAE 2 title! As Joan says, "Rally offers a relaxed atmosphere and less precise rules." Unfortunately, some people still show before they are ready—even with rally's relatively easy entry into dog sports.

Joan's big dogs enjoy rally because it is fast moving, and they are kept involved and focused. Tight turns can be a challenge with a giant breed, and remembering to leave space so that you don't wipe out cones or signs is important. Heeling is one of her dog's favorite exercises, as they do love to move. Sitting is generally not a big favorite of the larger dogs, and the Call Front, 1, 2, 3 Steps Backward is boring and way too repetitive for her dog to enjoy.

Joan's favorite sign is the Off-Set Figure 8—a sign where her dog can just keep on moving and where good attention is important. Her least-favorite signs are the 360-Degree Turns, which require a lot of bending when you are a Newfoundland. Sometimes course design does not take into consideration the space required for a large dog to perform easily. Luckily, Joan's dogs do agility as well, so they are very physically fit.

Rally did force Joan to change some of her training. "For obedience, I previously just trained one finish—now I have to train both because both appear in rally exercises." She has had to be careful not to talk too much when she switches into the obedience ring as well! Joan especially enjoys doing the Rally T challenge—a time limit on the course, and each exhibitor only gets one chance to walk the course. You really need to know your signs to do that well.

For newcomers to the sport of rally, Joan suggests, "Train with someone so that you can get help if you need it. Go to matches and run-throughs before you show if possible. Read the rules!" Luckily, because Novice is all on lead, you can't go too wrong even if you feel nervous and unprepared.

As a judge, Joan feels the most common mistake is trying to fix problems at the sign instead of reapproaching. You lose plenty of points repeating commands, while a retry may just cost you three points and help you refocus your dog.

Looking at a rally course with all of those signs and cones packed into a fairly small space, it seems that having a large breed of dog could be a handicap. "There are lots of pluses to having a big dog though—more to love, it doesn't matter at outdoor trials if the grass is long and not mowed, etc. The drawbacks include having to lug BIG crates and having some courses designed too tightly for a big dog." Joan's successes speak for themselves, though.

Competition and Beyond

Halt
Down
Walk Around
Dog

Preparing for a Trial

12

Now that your dog is trained, you are probably looking forward to entering at a trial and competing for titles and awards. While it is not necessary to compete at trials to enjoy rally, most people find that they enjoy the competition. You are spending the day with your dog and with other people who love dogs, and it can be a fun challenge.

Register Your Dog

You must make sure that your dog is registered with the organization and venue you wish to compete under. For the AKC, this means that your dog needs either an official AKC registration, complete with number or a Purebred Alternate Listing (PAL) or Indefinite Listing Privilege (ILP) number for a dog whose parentage you aren't sure of but who appears to be a purebred. Mixed-breed dogs can compete under the AKC's Canine Partners program. The WWKC and CKC only allow purebred dogs. The APDT and CARO allow all dogs to be entered at their competitions. The ASCA allows mixed breeds and purebreds other than Australian Shepherds to compete at their events, but you must have a "tracking" number or registration. You can go to the websites for these organizations (see Resources) to print out the needed forms. A fee will be required, but this is once for the lifetime of the dog.

Rally Speak

When discussing competing with their dogs, you will hear people talk about trials and matches. A trial is a formal competition, with strict rules and guidelines. Qualifying at a trial leads to titles that you can write after your dog's name. A match is a practice trial. It is a training situation in which you see if you and your dog are really ready for the "big time."

Know the Rules

Once your dog is registered, be sure that you are familiar with the rules for the venue you plan to enter. For example, the AKC allows chain slip collars but the APDT does not. You don't want to show up at the Start sign with an improper collar! Check the rules about leashes; whether or not you can carry food, and if you can carry food, when you are allowed to use it; and any rules about luring, physical encouragement, such as clapping, and verbal encouragement, such as chirping or whistling. Each organization has its own rules, and you may need to review them the day of the trial as well to be sure that they are fresh in your mind.

Rules can be downloaded from organization websites or ordered for a small fee. It can be helpful to print out a set of rules or order a small rulebook to bring with you to the trial in case you have questions before your run and don't get a chance to ask the judge. Your rally instructor may have rulebooks for sale or might organize a group order for your class to get a discount.

Participate in Matches

If possible, try to participate in some matches before you enter an official trial. A match is a practice trial. The conditions will be similar to a real trial, but often the judging is looser and you are given some leeway to train if you need to. Many match judges will offer advice or help guide you if you get stuck somewhere.

Matches can be crowded—this walk-through has plenty of handlers.

There are different types of matches. Some matches are truly run just like an official trial and will even give out ribbons—although qualifying runs will not count for titles. This means that you need to stay until the end for any ribbons or awards you may have earned.

Other matches are run-throughs or show-n-go's. In these cases, you are paying for the chance to run a course with someone who will judge and/or give you some tips, but you are not given a score or put in line for placements or qualifying ribbons. The plus to run-throughs is that, once your run is over, you are done and can leave. Many matches allow you to do multiple entries so that you can practice a course twice or even three times.

Most matches, run-throughs, and show-n-go's allow you to enter the day of the event. Others require a pre-entry. Some events give a discount if you pre-enter but also allow entries on the day of the event.

At matches, a knowledgeable judge will stop you when you perform an exercise incorrectly and guide you through it correctly. The judge may offer other tips to help you when you go to a "real" trial.

Matches are excellent places for both you and your dog to get over any performance jitters. You are exposed to many of the same conditions of a real trial, such as the noise, other dogs, people with food, and other distractions. Your dog is being asked to work and focus in a new and strange environment.

While you will undoubtedly be a bit nervous, your nerves will probably be better than when you try to earn titles. This way, you can feel out the best approach for you and your dog. Should you arrive very early and walk around to calm both of you down? Perhaps your dog will work best if he comes directly out of his crate and goes to the ring. Too much warm-up may make him dull and unenthused. Use trial and error to find which approach makes the most sense for you and your dog.

Attending matches will also help you figure out exactly what you need to pack and bring with you. It can help to develop a checklist to keep in your car.

Find Out About Upcoming Rally Events

How do you find out about upcoming rally events? The venues will have an event calendar on their websites. Click on a certain event to get the premium list. This is a small pamphlet that tells you exactly when and where the competition will be held, the fees required, and who will be judging. It will include an entry form for you to fill out. The entry form is sent to the organizers of the trial. (Note: Some trials allow entries on the day of the trial, but many require pre-entries—entries that must be sent in ahead of time. Be sure to check out all of the dates on the form so that your entry is sent in on time.)

If you are in a rally class, your instructor may have premiums for you to take or at least know about upcoming events, including matches and run-throughs.

Decide if You're Ready

How will you know if you and your dog really are ready for competition in the "big time," the "real thing"? Your instructor can help. She will let you know if she feels that you look ready to compete. And you can evaluate yourselves as well.

Do you understand the signs for your level of rally? Can you and your dog perform the signs at least reasonably well? It is even better if you can perform those signs very well at practice, at a match, or in class, as the real trial will be filled with more distractions for your dog and more nerves for you! Does your dog have good attention while heeling and working? Has he been "proofed' against common distractions, such as a loudspeaker, dogs working in the ring next to you, etc.? What about a judge in the ring with you or people applauding for other exhibitors? Your dog should be listening to you and working with you even if other dogs are barking, doors are opening and closing, or car horns are beeping. If the trial is indoors, hopefully you have trained indoors. The same goes for training and trialing outside. There are different distractions in both areas. Outdoors, you could face birds, revving motorcycles, horseback riders, bicycle riders, etc.—all things we have encountered at events.

While you can hopefully evaluate your dog, it is nice to have someone evaluate you! Do you understand the rules and regulations? Are you comfortable with all of the signs and with figuring out what you need to do on the fly? Is your footwork solid and consistent? You may even want your instructor to run you through a course without your dog to see how well you do.

Examine your expectations. If you are a perfectionist, then don't enter a trial until you are "super ready." You might even want to set a standard for yourself, such as you won't enter until you have earned a perfect score at three matches or practice run-throughs. You don't want to feel disappointed in your dog and yourself if you only earn a 99! Judges score differently, and some are tougher than others.

Does your dog have great attention, like this Corgi?

We say that, in dog sports, there are "gimmes and gotchas." A "gimme" is the day the judge decided that your tight lead really wasn't worth a point off and you got a 100. A "gotcha" is the day you are sure you did sign #10 correctly but the judge has you down for a three-point error. There is no sense in arguing—judges rarely change their scores. Just try to remember the "gimme," forget the "gotchas," and know that in the long run, they even out.

Your goal should be to complete the course, hopefully qualifying, but realizing that—no matter what—you and your dog had the chance to spend some wonderful time together. Your dog has no idea if he scored a 20 or a 100—all he knows is that he was lucky to have had some special time with you.

Some people enter a trial even before they feel completely ready. This may be to get a feel for where they need to work harder or where their dog has problems. This is fine—just adjust your expectations accordingly.

If you are in a class, don't feel pressured to enter a trial just because everyone else is. Each dog and handler team progresses at its own rate. You all have different backgrounds, and some teams may progress faster than others. Also, a confident dog may be ready well before a shy dog is. Know your own dog, and make the choices that are best for you as a team.

Fill Out the Entry Form

Once you get an entry form, review it carefully. The form will have the name of the sponsoring club, the date of the event, the fees, and where to send the form. For some events, you may enter online. Once you are sure that you have the correct form, fill it out. Most of the information required is self-explanatory. You will need your dog's birth date and breeder (if known), along with breed, sex, and registration number. You will have to fill in your name, address, and contact information. It is very important that you sign the disclaimer. The form will also tell you the exact fees and how to make out your check. Most events will also have a closing date listed. Your entry must be received before that date or it won't be accepted.

Figure Out Which Class to Enter

Figuring out which class to enter can be trickier. If neither you nor your dog has ever earned an obedience or rally title, then you can enter Novice A. Once either of you has earned an obedience or rally title, you must enter Novice B. So

Rally Caution

Many dog competitions will not allow a bitch in heat to compete. Most of the organizations will provide at least a partial refund but not all. Plan your entries around your dog's heat cycles if she is intact.

after your first dog has earned a rally title, you are no longer eligible for Novice A. Advanced A and Excellent A only look at your dog's accomplishments, not yours. So if your dog has no obedience titles, he can enter Advanced A rally even if you have put advanced rally titles on other dogs.

If this is your first dog competition, you will be in rally Novice or Level 1 and in the A class. If your dog has competed before in other rally venues or in other dog sports, you will need to check the rules. For example, a dog who has earned an obedience title through the AKC is required to enter Novice B rally.

Read the Premium List

The premium list will give directions to the trial site. You will not know the exact schedule of classes and start times until you receive confirmation from the club. The judging schedule will tell you the start time. Be sure that you pay attention to the walk-through times! Your dog's class may officially begin running at 9:00 a.m., but the walk-through may be from 8:40 a.m. to 8:50 a.m. You want to be sure that you arrive in time to do the walk-through, preferably even earlier so that your dog can relax and you can set up your crate, chair, etc. It is a good idea to allow extra time for the drive, too, in case you run into traffic problems or get lost.

Some trials will require a long drive and an overnight hotel stay. The premium list should include information on hotels near the trial site and which ones will allow dogs. Never leave your dog outside in your car overnight or at the trial site in his crate. Rally is a sport for you to do together, and it isn't fair to leave your partner.

Be aware of some basic hotel etiquette rules. If your dog is likely to leap on the bed, bring a sheet or cover for the bed. Most dogs do best with a crate in the room, especially if you plan to go out at all. If your dog is likely to bark if you are out of the room, he should not be left alone. It is not fair to the other guests, and complaints could cause the hotel management to ban dogs altogether.

Do not bathe or groom your dog in the hotel room. The added hair and possible plumbing damage could lead to a dog ban. Some clubs arrange with hotel managers to be contacted if a room is left in disgraceful shape and will fine you or report you to the overseeing organization, such as the AKC. Many hotels ask for a dog deposit and may refuse to return it if your room is messy.

Whenever traveling, be sure to pick up after your dog! Hotels, parks, and rest areas can quickly become gross messes if people leave dog poop. Not only that, but stool poses health hazards for both people and dogs. Many municipalities have hefty fines for those who do not clean up after their dogs.

Pack for the Trial

Okay, the forms are mailed in with the correct information and fees, and now you are getting ready for that first trial. Plan ahead so that you pack everything you might need for the competition. Plus, take along some basic equipment that travels everywhere your dog does.

Basics

- plastic bags for cleaning up poop
- crate or a special doggy seat belt so that your dog will be safe while traveling in your car
- first-aid kit
- health and emergency information on your dog—keep a copy of his rabies certificate in the glove compartment
- leash (a regular leash that is acceptable for showing, a retractable for other situations)
- make sure that your dog has some identification on him—tags, tattoo, and/or microchip
- medications you or your dog may possibly need, such as aspirin or an antihistamine

- treats for training, warming up, and rewarding
- water bowl and a large jug of water from home

Nice but not always necessary:

- chair for you
- cover for the crate for a dog who wants or needs some peace and quiet
- fan for hot weather
- separate crate that folds and is lightweight to carry to put near the ring

When you are entered in a trial or match, you may want to pack a few extra items.

This dog and handler look neat and well groomed and are even in step!

Trial/Match Packing

- correct equipment for your dog—the right collar and lead, depending on the venue
- rulebook for that venue
- brush, comb, or cloth to be sure that your dog looks his best
- trial confirmation sheet and directions
- appropriate outerwear for you
- nice outfit to show in—this doesn't need to be fancy, but make sure that you look neat and clean and that you have comfortable and sensible shoes
- notebook that records your training notes, achievements, etc. While not necessary, this can be helpful for the future to see what mistakes you made, what you need to work on, any comments about the judge or the course, etc. You may also want to keep your course maps in a folder for future practice.

Many exhibitors find it simplest to have a trial bag that is kept packed all the time so that you know exactly where your trial lead and collar are. With one tote or bag for everything, it is much easier for you to get established at a trial site. You will still have to carry the crate separately, and possibly a chair, but the workload is less. Many exhibitors with larger dogs invest in a luggage cart or dolly on which to pack all of their supplies, including crate and chair.

Dress Nicely

Be aware that you are not permitted to wear anything into the ring that identifies the group you train with, your dog, or you.

Always assume the worst when it comes to weather and outdoor trials. Be prepared for rain, snow, heat, and humidity. Hopefully, you have accustomed your dog to working with you, even if you are wearing a long coat or a wide-brimmed hat. The judge will be sensibly dressed for the weather too, so it is a nice idea to have your dog used to other people around the ring in unusual outfits. Always pack sensible shoes. This is not the time for stiletto heels, flip flops, or mountain-climbing boots. For indoor trials, dark shoes are a good idea, and for outdoors, shoes with good traction soles are ideal, in case the grass is wet.

Dress neatly and sensibly for the rally ring.

Some obedience competitors stress that you should dress with slacks that match the color of your dog. For example, if you have a black Labrador Retriever, you would wear black pants and black shoes. By matching the color of your pants and shoes to your dog, lack-of-precision errors are less conspicuous. This is more important in competitive obedience, where even a slightly crooked *sit* may mean a half point off. Still, even for rally, it can't hurt.

Most organizations will not let you compete while wearing a shirt or jacket with your dog's name on it. So although you can wear a nice shirt with an Australian Shepherd embroidered, you can't wear one with that says "Great Dog Kangaroo Hunter CDX RAE."

I feel that it is a sign of respect for your dog and the judge for you to arrive at the ring looking neat and clean, and with your dog well groomed. You are representing your breed, your club, or the instructor you train with, and the sport of dogs. Do us proud!

Have a Support Group

If you have friends who will be at the trial, you may want to make arrangements to crate near to them. Having a support group can be wonderful, whether you need it for consolation or celebration.

Some people prefer a quiet time when they come out of the ring to commune with their dog, think over their run, walk a bit to relax, etc. This may not be a good time for someone, no matter how well intentioned, to come over and point out a major error she made or give tips on how to do better. In fact, sometimes it is best to simply write down tips or hints and give them to a competitor later. Very often, someone knows if she made a silly mistake and she doesn't need or want a lot of reminders. By the same token, if you don't want a commentary on your run right after it, simply tell people, "Not right now please."

Rally Profile

Deb Eldredge and My Real Rally Experience

The AKC started their rally program on January 1, 2005.

Arrival in Rochester, New York is set for 10 p.m. on Friday, December 31. We had six dogs and three people in the mini van: two Pembroke Welsh Corgis, two Australian Shepherds, and two Belgian Tervurens.

Things are a bit hectic for the first trial—more than 100 people needing numbers, Novice A vs. Novice B situations being straightened out, and walk-throughs starting. The course is basically easy and straightforward. Novice A goes first, with 15 or so people. The first Novice A dog is an Italian Greyhound, the second is an Irish Wolfhound. Great sport! My son Tom with Baloo, the Australian Shepherd, gets the honor of being the first junior handler to earn a rally leg, and Baloo is the first Aussie to earn one. Almost everyone passes. The Novice B people go through quickly. Judge Nancy Withers is kind. Dottie, our instructor, is clearly a much tougher judge than these people, but she has trained us well. We all pass! My personal high point was the perfect 100 score by Hokey, my seven-month-old Tervuren pup.

The next morning, we're back for round two. Again, Novice A goes first. The second rally course is again reasonable and straightforward, although this judge is a bit tougher. There are many fewer 100s. For some reason, despite two different judges who presumably did not collaborate, the courses are remarkably similar. We persevere and virtually everyone passes again. The judge remarks that we must all train hard.

That night, Novice B is to go first. This means that Tom will kick his heels for three hours or so and then run. I am convinced that he will not pay attention to his course and will blow his big chance to put a rally title on Baloo. Dottie says that he will do fine. My daughter Kate has given up and settled in with a book. I watch and pace, more nervous when my kids run than when I run.

The final course is the most difficult. Now why, why would a judge do that? Judge Nancy Withers is a bit ill, and we speculate if that will make her judging easier or tougher. She demands Coke—"in the red cans, full sugar, full caffeine!" The Eldredge dogs are looking a bit tired, except, of course, for Super Puppy, who bounds out of his crate with enthusiasm. I am feeling older by the minute. Once again, most of us pass and the crowd flees, leaving only those with Novice A entries or friends to watch.

Tom is the grand finale and follows about three dogs after a dog who piddles on a sign. I feel cold fear, knowing that Baloo may try to add his two cents' worth to the comments on the floor. Nancy moves the signs over a bit. Tom and Baloo nearly wipe out the entire spiral but keep saving themselves by dramatic body movements, and they earn their title. I earn ten brand-new gray hairs.

Amazingly, all six Eldredge dogs sport new RNs—from almost 13-year-old Susan, the Pembroke Welsh Corgi, to 7-month-old Hokey, the Tervuren pup. Due to the insane scheduling and luck of the running order, we have a number of "firsts" as well. First Pembroke Welsh Corgi to Susan, first Belgian Tervuren to Hokey, first Junior to earn a leg to Tom, first Junior to earn a title to Kate, first Australian Shepherd to earn a leg to Baloo, first Australian Shepherd to earn a title to Tia, first tracking titled dog to Flash. Not bad for about 36 hours of sheer madness!

5
Left
Turn

Competing in Your First Trial

13

The big day has finally arrived—you are heading off to your first real rally trial! Be sure that you have planned your day out carefully. Have the directions in hand or already packed in the car. Get up early enough to walk and feed your dog before leaving home. Some dogs do better without breakfast—you'll learn what works best for your individual dog. Many dogs will not eliminate, at least not poop, when away from home. So be sure that you are up early enough to give him a good walk.

Ideally, you packed your car the night before so that you are ready to go when your dog is set. Having a quick checklist can be a good idea, especially for the first couple of times you trial so that you don't forget anything. You may want to ask your instructor to look over your list in case you forgot to write down something essential.

Put your dog into his safe travel arrangement—whether a crate or seat belt—and off you go!

This Corgi has her bag packed and her seatbelt on!

Before a Trial

You need to do a little homework before you head out to your first trial. This means checking over your premium list carefully, possibly talking to friends or an instructor who has competed at this site before, or even calling the club up if you have questions. You want to be as prepared as possible to make this a wonderful outing for you and your dog.

Find Out Where Dogs Can Be Crated

When you get to the trial site, find out where dogs can be crated. If outdoors, look for a shady spot. Indoors, you may want a quiet corner where your dog can rest without a lot of distraction. Locate the potty area for the dogs and the bathroom for you.

Check Out the Rings

Check out the rings, especially if there are multiple rings, so that you will know where you will be competing. Then move your dog's equipment into the spot you have chosen. Be sure to bring in his water and a bowl. Once you have

Rally Caution

Your dog should never be off lead at a trial except when he is in the ring competing. Some trials ban the use of retractable leads on the trial site as well. This is for everyone's safety.

everything set up, get your dog out and give him another walk. You may want to walk around the trial site so that he can check things out. Do not go into the rings, however—that is not allowed.

Check In

When your dog has settled into his new home for a day, go back to your ring to check in and pick up your number. The steward will give you an armband for your left arm. Generally, rubber bands are also provided to hold the armband in place. Some competitors purchase or make special armband holders with a Velcro strap to hold their numbers.

Do a Walk-Through

This is a good time to find out about the walk-through and make sure that you can be there to walk the course. Remember your sequencing training! (See Chapter 11.) I suggest a minimum of three walk-throughs per course. First, do a quick walk-through just to find and follow the numbers. This will give you a feel for the flow of the course. Make sure that you follow the numbers exactly, and don't skip any stations! After that first quick walk, go slowly the second time through. Read each sign carefully—getting the right finish in your mind on Recall signs, turns correct, etc. If you are reading the signs correctly, one sign should lead you to the next.

Then do a third walk-through. This time, go through the actual exercises, just as if your dog was with you. Almost everyone else will be doing this too—even saying the commands to their "invisible" dogs out loud, so you won't look out of place. It may also help to stand quietly in the center of the course and follow it with just your eyes. This may help really establish the course flow in your mind.

Don't be afraid to practice your signals as you walk the course.

Double-Check the Signs

Hopefully, you packed your rulebook so that you can double-check any signs you have questions about. A rulebook is often available at the check-in desk as well, but you can only use this one at ringside.

Pay Attention to the Briefing

The judge will do a briefing at some point, either before or after the walk-through. This is the time for you to ask any questions you have. Does the judge want certain exercises performed before or after the sign? When should the next dog be ready to enter the ring? Remember that, especially for the Novice A or Level 1 A classes, everyone is a beginner. The judge will try to give you advice and encouragement. She may explain a sign or two to ensure that the correct execution of that exercise is clear in everyone's mind. Undoubtedly, she will remind you to be positive, have fun, and enjoy your dog.

Check the Poster Board

Near the entrance to the ring is a big poster board or dry erase board. On this board are the numbers of all of the entries, often with the breed of dog listed as well. When people check in, a single line is run through the number. Then, once a team has entered the ring, a second line is made to "X" out the number. This board is your guide for the day. You can check it to see how many dogs run before you. In Novice, figure no more than one minute per team—some will be faster, some slower. Generally, estimate that you need to be near the ring entrance about three or four dogs before your turn. It helps if you have an unusual breed as your marker—say a Plott Hound. If you are at a breed specialty, this gets trickier, as you may be the 20th Pembroke Welsh Corgi after 19 other Pembroke Welsh Corgis!

Check to See How Many Dogs Have Run

Once the class has started, periodically check to see how many dogs have already gone. Check frequently because some people may arrive late to check in or others may be absent. The judge can only wait so long if you are late getting to the ring, as you are holding up all of the other exhibitors of the day. If you are nervous, be sure to plan in extra time so that you can make a quick dash to the bathroom.

For a rough idea, figure on about two minutes per dog for each run. Plus add in 10 minutes for a walk-through and 10 to 15 minutes for the judge's briefing and for the judge to figure scores at the end of a class. If your class runs after a lunch break, generally that will be another 30 to 45 minutes to add in. It is easiest if your class has an actual start time, but Novice is often toward the end of the day and may simply be marked "to follow." These time estimates give you a guide, but realize that if the weather is bad, exhibitors may have chosen not to come or could be delayed due to traffic.

You may end up first or within the first four dogs in your class. In that case, pay attention at the judge's briefing. The judge will generally give a time for any more walk-throughs and then say when she wants the first dog on the line at the gate. It may be as short as five minutes, so you might need to go get your dog right away and give him a quick warm-up.

Warm Up Your Dog

Deciding how much warm-up your dog needs takes practice. Some dogs do best coming out of their crate and going directly into the ring. Most dogs fare better with a bit of practice before they go in—perhaps some short heeling patterns, a few turns, and maybe a Recall or Finish. Don't bore your dog with too many repetitions. An older dog may need a few stretches to warm up tight muscles. Our older Corgi had about six *sits* per day in her repertoire, so her warm-up didn't include any *sits* because I needed to "save" those *sits* for her course! A young dog may need some extra time to walk around and adjust to all of the distractions. Hopefully, you were able to try different warm-up patterns with your dog at some matches before the trial.

Inspect Yourself

Before you enter the ring, do a quick check of you! You can't have any treats (in AKC competition and the later levels of the APDT) or toys on you or in your pockets, and no bait bags or fanny packs are allowed. You should not have a cell phone or pager with you during your run. If you approach the ring and realize that you have treats or a toy with you, simply ask a fellow exhibitor to hold them for you until after your run.

Observe the Other Participants

Often, the Novice B or Level 1 B will run first, then the A classes. This is very nice because it gives you a chance to watch some of the more experienced teams run first. Most experienced handlers are very open to giving you hints and training tips once their run is over. Do not try to question someone right before she enters the ring. She is trying to concentrate on the course and her dog.

During a Trial

Once you enter the ring, you are on your own almost at once. The judge will usually ask if you are ready. Then she will give you the command to start. You now go at your own pace, moving forward based on the path your signs take you. Do not feel hurried! Most dogs can easily make any time limits. Go along at a comfortable pace for both of you, although brisk is often better because your dog has less time to check out distractions. Make sure to leave enough space so that neither you nor your dog knocks over signs or cones.

This cute mixed breed is off and running on her APDT course.

Remember that you are allowed to give verbal encouragement and hand signals. You can even talk to yourself and no one will care! Luring is allowed in some venues, and patting your leg can encourage a dog who tends to lag. Feel free to chirp, cheep, or even meow. Your goal is to keep your dog with you, have your leash loose, and perform the signs correctly and in the right order. Plus, have fun!

If you make a mistake, remember to start over and do the entire exercise again. For example, if your dog goes directly to *heel* position on a Recall exercise, start back at the Recall part. So collect your dog, get his attention, and then back up to call him again, this time with a *sit* reminder as he comes in front. Small errors, such as sitting crookedly in front, are generally not worth repeating the exercise. Take the deduction and move on. Luckily, you do not need a perfect score, or 100, or 200 to earn a leg or a title.

After a Trial

As you leave the ring, don't forget to tell your dog what a big star he was. No matter what, he tried to do the course correctly—if he had problems, it simply shows you where you need to work harder in your training. Give him a good petting, possibly some treats, or some playtime with a toy, and then back to his crate. Make sure that he has fresh water to drink because having to concentrate can make him thirsty. You may need a drink too! Then you may want to head back to the ring to see how you did.

When you have finished your run, the judge will record the time and the desk steward will add up your score. The score, but not your time, will be written on the board that lists the running order. So, within a few minutes after your run you will know if you qualified and how well you did.

At the end of the class, the judge will call all of the teams that qualified back into the ring. She will then give out a qualifying ribbon to each team. The top teams receive placements and additional ribbons. In the AKC, all qualifying teams receive a green ribbon. In the APDT, the trial hosting club can choose the color it wants for the qualifying ribbons. Qualifying ribbons are generally flat. On the qualifying ribbon will be the name of the host club, the date of the trial, the judge, and your score. This information may be added via a sticky label, and you may need to fill in some of the information yourself. This is a good way to keep track of your accomplishments, and the ribbon provides proof of your accomplishment in case there is a question or paperwork gets lost.

After the awards for the class are given out, most judges are open to questions or letting you look at your score sheet to see where you had errors. Give the judge a chance to unwind a bit first before you approach. She may need a quick bathroom run or a drink on a hot day. If another class follows directly, she may need to set up the next course, but you can then ask her your questions while the next group does their walk-through. Even if you disagree, always be respectful and polite. Remember, you chose to enter and paid for the judge's opinion. If you decide that you don't like that opinion, simply don't enter under

Rally Speak

You will hear competitors talk about their dogs earning "legs." Each time your dog qualifies at a real trial, he has earned a "leg" toward his title. Most titles require three "legs."

that judge again. Judges are human and may be tired, sick, or simply having a bad day. Still, most judges try very hard to be helpful, especially to novice exhibitors.

Many rally exhibitors will also purchase a special book to keep track of their rally accomplishments. (See the Resources.) This book will record your successes and failures and help you see what areas of training you need more work in. You can make your own book simply by designating a small notebook for your rally training and trialing.

An example of an AKC Rally® title certificate.

To earn a title, your dog must complete the course on three separate occasions. Some venues, such as those sponsored by the AKC, require three different judges, while others, like those of the APDT, will allow two different judges. You must at least attempt all of the exercises, you can't skip any signs, and you must earn a minimum score. The score varies with the venue. For the AKC, you must earn at least 70 out of 100. In the APDT, the minimum score is 170 out of 200.

Once the organization has processed all of the trial entries, you will receive a certificate or notification in the mail. Now you can add those letters to the back of your dog's name! In the AKC, that would mean Spot is now Spot RN for Rally Novice. In the APDT, Spot is now Spot RL-1 for Rally Level 1.

If you and your dog have had a wonderful run, you might even be in the running for a placement. Placements are generally given out to the top four dogs, although in the APDT, the top five earn an extra ribbon.

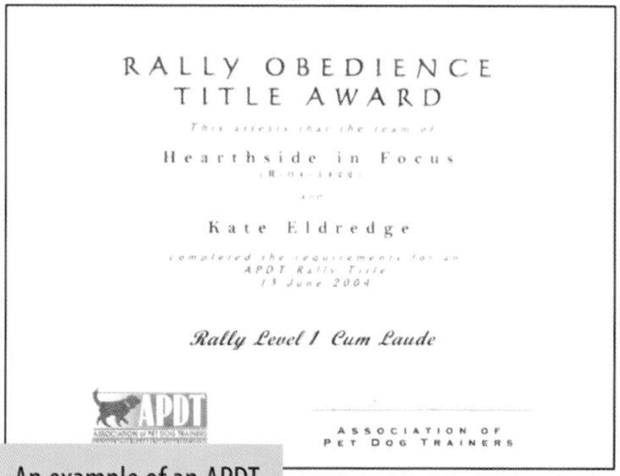

An example of an APDT rally title certificate.

Placements

Once your dog has earned a rally title, you may want to purchase a pin or patch to commemorate the occasion. Pins can be worn by you when you compete, and a patch can be sewn onto your jacket or onto the trial bag you bring with you to events. Once your certificate arrives, you may want to frame it and put it in a prominent place in your house. After all, you and your dog earned that title together! While it may not be quite as imposing as a law school diploma, it still represents a significant accomplishment.

There will be days when you fly home, barely needing any gas for your car due to your brilliant dog and your wonderful success. Other days, you may feel like creeping home, head buried in embarrassment or overwhelmed with discouragement. You should not feel that way! Whatever mistakes you and your dog have made, others have undoubtedly made the same mistake at some time too. Trust me—it can't get much worse than watching your large male Kuvasz effortlessly jump in and out of a number of obedience rings after deciding that heeling was way too boring.

Scoring

Because rally is a judged event with placements and titles being earned, you are being scored. Each venue has its own scoring system, but the two major ones are the AKC and the APDT. For the AKC, you must earn a score of 70 or better out of a possible 100 points. For the APDT, you must earn a score of 170 or better out of a possible 200 points.

For both organizations, some errors will cause you to fail no matter what your score. Any dog who eliminates (urinating or defecating) in the ring will be excused, as well as any dog who vomits in the ring. If you totally miss a sign and never attempt it, you will fail. That will also happen if you do exercises out of order, which is also called an "off course."

A dog who is aggressive toward people or other dogs will be asked to leave. If your lead is tight the entire time in a Novice or Level 1 run, the judge may give you a nonqualifying score. The same can be true of nonstop or uncontrolled barking. If your dog decides that he does not want to play on a given day and leaves the ring, you will be eliminated.

Many of the other nonqualifying scores are due to problems with the jumps in upper levels. If your dog knocks a bar down or doesn't clear the entire broad jump, you will not qualify. You are not allowed to simply replace the bar or board and try again. You also may not touch your dog except when specifically allowed in the exercise descriptions.

Donna, with her Aussie Click and her Greyhound Vinnie, had a successful rally weekend.

The APDT has a number of other specific nonqualifying faults. These include passing on opposite sides of a cone, exceeding the maximum course time of four minutes, using food treats incorrectly, and any time a dog-and-handler team loses ten or more points on an exercise. In the AKC, you can totally fail an exercise (which is a ten-point deduction) but still pass if your score is over 70.

Luring or even the appearance of luring is frowned upon in the APDT and can result in failure. Ask the judge during the handler briefing what hand positions they consider to give the appearance of luring so that you can avoid making that mistake.

In general, errors must be worth at least a point before they are deducted. So if your dog does a slightly crooked *sit*, which might mean a half-point off in obedience, that error will not be scored against you in rally.

One-Point Errors

Common one-point errors include:

- a tight leash
- hitting but not knocking over a jump
- a slow response by your dog so that you need multiple commands to get him to obey
- being out of position—lagging or forging on heeling, sitting crooked, heeling

Rally Profile

Cindy and Patriot

The team of Cindy Warner and her stunning Shetland Sheepdog Patriot are generally acknowledged to be one of the top teams in rally in upstate New York. But Cindy started with rally as a "repair" for her obedience work with Patriot.

"I started training in rally in October, 2004. Patriot had one leg toward his Open title in obedience (the CDX), but we were suddenly failing time after time. Both of us were discouraged. Rally sounded like a nice break from the stress of obedience while still allowing both of us to attend trials and compete. It worked out beautifully!" For Patriot, some of the stress in obedience came from worrying about where the judge was and the judge following the team on exercises like their heelwork. With rally, even if the judge kept following, Cindy could reassure him with "happy talk" and praise while he worked. Rally also moves right along, which helped Patriot to focus on Cindy and keep going.

Cindy offers some advice to people interested in rally as a sport. "Your dog should know basic obedience before you start rally. Sit, down, come, and heel are important. Read the rules and regulations, and make sure that you are familiar with the signs. If you hesitate on course, you will lose time and your dog may feel confused. Try to hit matches or run-throughs before you enter a real trial."

wide, or perhaps touching you while heeling

- minor movements on the Stand exercises

If some of those errors are major rather than minor, such as your dog sitting behind you on a finish instead of at *heel* position, you might lose more than just one point.

Three-Point Errors

The next grouping is the three-point errors. These include:

- having to retry a station
- knocking over a cone or sign in the AKC—that means you or your dog!
- loud or rough commands
- lack of teamwork—perhaps you don't move together on a pivot
- handler stepping inside the 6-foot (1.2 m) line when the dog jumps in Level 2 of the APDT

Five-Point Errors

The APDT also has a list of standard five-point deductions. These include:

- knocking over a cone or sign
- an incorrect finish
- dog not sitting, downing, or standing as required
- performing an exercise backward or in the opposite direction—such as doing an Inside Spiral with the dog on the outside

Those of us who choose to compete with our dogs deserve extra credit for our efforts. We are working in a team sport with another species. When people compete with their horse or their dairy cow or whatever else, at all times someone has a restraint or hold on that animal. But with our dogs, there comes a moment when we trust that our bond of love and our hours of training will act as an invisible leash. Sometimes we may be a bit premature in our thinking. Still, with time, clever training, patience, and love, there will be a day when the leash comes off, the dog looks Velcroed to our side, and we succeed beyond our wildest dreams. I can only hope that you have many of those days!

14 Nonregular Classes and Bonuses

As soon as rally became a titling venue in the AKC, people started thinking of unique and fun ways to utilize the rally format. This has led to the formation of a number of nonregular rally classes. These classes can be offered at AKC trials, but they do not lead to any official titles. While nonregular classes do not lead to titles, placements do not depend on having a qualifying score. The four best teams get placements even if the performances left something to be desired! We will go over AKC nonregular classes first, then cover APDT Bonuses at the end of the chapter.

Rally Pairs

One of the first nonregular rally classes to be proposed was Rally Pairs. In this competition, the team consists of one handler and two dogs. No jumps are used, and the rules do not require that both dogs be of the same breed. You perform the course just as you would with one dog, only now you have a pair—both on the left side and in *heel* position. This class can be offered at any level from Novice to Excellent. Obviously, the course design takes into consideration that extra spacing is needed for the extra width of another dog.

Rally Caution

Doing well in a nonregular class will not count toward a title, although the classes are usually fun and challenging.

In this class, the total score is 200 points, as you might lose points for just one dog on an exercise. For example, on a Halt Sit, one dog might sit while the other one remains standing.

Rally Team

This is a class for four handlers, each with one dog. It may be offered at any level from Novice to Excellent. Each individual dog and handler team runs the course separately. Timing is crucial here. The timing starts when the first dog and handler get the *forward* command from the judge, and timing doesn't end until the last dog and handler team passes the Finish sign.

Performances are scored for each exercise by each team, with a perfect score of 400 available for the team. Jumps are not included, as teams may have dogs of different jump heights.

Rally Plus

This nonregular class is clearly intended as a stepping stone from rally to novice obedience. Scoring is based on a perfect score of 200. The course is performed off lead. The start of the course is 180 to 200 feet (55 to 61 m) of linear heeling. Handlers are allowed to talk freely, encouraging their dogs until they reach the first cone or marker indicating a distance of 3 feet (1 m) past the first turn. Once the team reaches the Halt Sit sign, the handler may again begin to use verbal encouragement and praise.

The course has 20 to 25 stations, including 7 stationary exercises. One of those exercises is the Halt, Stand, and Walk Around. In this class, that exercise is modified a bit. The handler stands the dog, then walks 3 to 6 feet (1 to 2 m) away in front of the dog. The judge will come up and do the Quick Stand for Exam done in novice obedience, touching the dog on the head, shoulders, or body and hindquarters. As the judge finishes, the handler goes around the dog, returning to heel with a pause and then continuing on the course.

A team doing the quiet heeling.

When the course is finished, the time stops but your work doesn't. The handler takes her dog to a designated spot in the ring and leaves him in a *sit-stay*. She walks to the end of the ring, turns, and calls her dog. This can be verbal, a hand signal, or both. Two attempts are allowed before any points are deducted. Once the dog sits in front, the handler then signals or uses a verbal command or both to get the dog to finish. All of this is done without any direction from the judge.

For the grand finale, the dog-and-handler

team must perform a one-minute Honor *sit-stay*. So after the Recall, the team goes to an "honor" spot. The dog will be left there in a *sit-stay* while the handler goes about 15 feet (4.5 m) away, then turns to face her dog. Meanwhile, the next dog is getting ready to run. A steward will time the dog doing the *sit-stay* for one minute. At the end of the minute, the handler will return, quietly put the leash on her dog, and leave the ring.

Competing in this class could be an excellent way to judge whether you and your dog are ready to take the big step into formal obedience. It is a real blend of rally and obedience and requires a variety of skills.

Rally T Challenge

Rally T challenge is truly designed as a test of your rally skills and teamwork. The "T" stands for time. The judge walks her own course three times, timing each walk. Then she takes the average of the three walks and adds five seconds for each stationary exercise. Any dog and handler team that goes over the maximum allowed course time is penalized one point for each second over time. A fast team will gain a point for every second under course time.

A perfect score in this class is 200, although a fast team may actually score over 200. The signs for Rally Advanced plus some special Rally T Challenge signs may be used. The course is performed off lead.

Adding to the "Challenge" part is that each handler is given the chance to do one walk-through of the course. This must be a straight walk, without actually practicing any of the signs. (If you practice a sign you receive an automatic five-point penalty.)

Rally T Challenge Signs

The signs and exercises described below are specific for the Rally T Challenge class and won't be seen on any other courses in the AKC.

Halt, Slow Forward From Sit

For this sign, you and your dog will heel up to the sign, which will be on your righthand side. You stop and your dog sits in *heel* position. When you move forward, you must go at a slow pace. This sign will either end a course or be followed by a Normal Pace sign. The Normal sign is a fast forward from the *sit*.

Halt, 90-Degree Pivot Right, Forward

This sign will be placed directly in front of you because you will be changing direction. You heel up to this sign and halt with your dog sitting in the *heel* position.

Queezle is in the *sit* and Kate is using a treat to lure her into the pivot right.

And they turn and go!

You then pivot to the right (remember those 3 "Ps:" plant your feet, pie plate space, and partners) with your dog and move directly on. The Standard sign has your dog sit directly after the pivot; here your dog will *not* sit after the pivot.

This sign has your dog on the outside, so he will have to hustle to stay in position, especially because you will be moving right off.

Halt, 90-Degree Pivot Left, Forward

This asks for the reverse of the previous sign. You approach the sign directly with your dog. He sits when you halt, then you pivot together to the left and move off immediately.

Your dog should not sit after the pivot. With this sign, he is on the inside and may have to back up to stay in position as you pivot and before you move off.

Leave Dog, 2 Steps, Call to Heel—Forward

This sign comes up on your right. You and your dog will heel up to the sign. You stop and your dog sits in *heel* position. Tell your dog to stay, using a verbal cue,

Kate uses the leash behind her back and a treat to swing Queezle into the left pivot.

a hand signal, or both. You take two steps forward, then pause and call your dog to heel as you move forward.

Your dog will have to move quickly to catch up to you because you are already two steps ahead of him, plus you are now moving away. Many dogs feel that exercises like this are fun, though—they love to "catch" you!

Rally Speak

Remember, whenever a sign calls for a "Front," it means that your dog must come and sit straight right in front of you. There is always a *sit* required.

Call Front, 1 Step Diagonal Right, Front, Finish Right, Forward

Okay, you may feel exhausted just reading the sign! You and your dog are heeling forward when you step backward and call him to front. He will sit in front. Once he is sitting, take one step backward on a diagonal to your right. Your dog should come with you as you move and sit again in front at the new location. Now signal your dog to finish to the right, using a verbal cue, hand signal, or both. As soon as your dog is moving, head forward so that he does not

Sara has left Echo and will now call her to heel.

Echo hustles to catch up.

Rally Profile

Susan, Whisper, Kiss, Logan, Cane, and Bonnet

Susan comes to rally trials with her squad of Belgian Malinois. These athletic dogs work precisely and happily, enjoying the sport of rally. All five of Susan's dogs have titled in rally, from ARCHX in the APDT to RAE titles in the AKC.

Susan started with rally back in 2003, doing APDT before the AKC started up its program. She felt that rally would be a good foundation for obedience. "Rally gives confidence to the young or inexperienced dog (and handler, too) in a show setting." Her youngest dog, Cane, has certainly benefitted from training and competing in rally.

Her Malinois seem to note the signs right away and realize that they are doing rally. The variation in exercises is fun for them, and they don't mind the lack of flow that may bother some dogs. Because Susan had an obedience background, training her dogs the basics for the exercises was simple and easy. Learning to drop from a stand was the trickiest new task for her experienced dogs. She is now teaching that move to her young dogs right from the start.

For Susan, rally training and competition has been a training tool for obedience. "I do request precision right from the start. I think that rally has helped keep my dogs interested in obedience, as it offers more variety with the many exercises."

Susan's advice to anyone starting in rally is to be sure that your dog has some basic obedience training first and knows the main commands. "When I enter, I want the dog prepared and to have a good chance to get that top score. Going in with an untrained dog is a waste of time, as you still have to deal with the show environment, the judge, and unusual events around you. It is a great way to give a green dog show experience."

sit when he gets back to *heel* position.

This will require a bit of speed and dexterity on the part of your dog.

Call Front, 1 Step Back Diagonal Left, Front, Finish Left, Forward

Once you have the previous sign mastered, this will hopefully come easily to you. This sign is the reverse of the previous one. You again back up, calling your dog. He will sit in front. Then you take a step backward but this time slanting your diagonal to the left. Your dog will—or should—move with you and sit in front again when you stop at your new location. Then tell him to finish to the left, using a verbal cue, hand signal, or both, and move right off so that he doesn't sit in *heel* position.

Double Left, About Turn

This is the rally course designer's final chance to make you totally dizzy. You will head into this sign and do your normal Left About Turn. Turn to the left while your dog goes to the right around you so that you end up together and in *heel* position, heading in the exact opposite direction from which you started. You can then take a step or two before you do another normal Left About Turn. So basically, you end up going in the same direction you were heading initially, after doing a lot of spinning around! You will have done a 360-degree turn to the left while your dog will have done a 360-degree turn to the right. You need to keep moving during this exercise so that your dog has no chance to sit. Most dogs think this is fun—most handlers are left feeling a bit dizzy.

APDT Bonus Exercises

In the APDT, a course may include a bonus exercise or two. These bonus signs are worth ten points if done perfectly. Those points will be added to your final score if you choose to do the bonus. So in the APDT, you could achieve a score of over 200 when the bonus is added. Different bonus signs are available for use at the different levels. Many of the bonus exercises can be thought of as "bridges" to obedience exercises.

Bonus exercises are done after your run is finished. So you pass the Finish sign and timing is stopped. You and your dog then go to where the bonus exercise is set up and attempt it. You need to let the judge know before you start your run if you want to try the bonus. You will not lose any points even if you fail the bonus. If you do it perfectly, you will gain ten points. If you have any points deducted, you will gain whatever you did earn.

Level 1

Halt, Leave Dog, Call to Heel: This bonus exercise uses two signs. The first sign is a simple Halt, Leave Dog. So you heel up to the sign, which will be on your right. Stop and your dog sits. Once your dog is sitting, either drop your leash or take it off. Then tell your dog to stay and walk by yourself to the next sign, which will say Call to Heel. Without turning around, call your dog to come up and sit in *heel* position. You may turn your head slightly, but you cannot turn around to face your dog. You can use a verbal cue, hand signal, or both as your cues. Once your dog is sitting, put the leash back on him or pick it up.

Call Dog Front, Side Step Right or Left: There are two versions of this sign: one sending you right for your side step and one sending you left for your side step. For both versions, you will be heeling with your dog and can then back up and call him to front. Once he is sitting, take a full step to either the right or left—your choice. Your dog is to move *with* you and sit in front again when you stop.

Halt, Leave Dog Recall, Turn and Call, Finish R/L: This is another two-sign bonus. For the first sign, you will see Halt, Leave Dog Recall. So you heel up to this sign and ask your dog to sit. Then remove your lead or leave it to drag. Walk forward to the second sign, which is about 10 feet (3 m) away. This sign says Turn and Call, Finish R/L. Turn at the sign so that you are now facing your dog, who is in a *stay* by the first sign. Call him and he should come and sit in front. Then tell him to finish. You can go either right or left—it is your choice.

Level 2

Moving Down, Leave Dog—(Turn) Call Front, Finish R/L: For the first sign, which is Moving Down, Leave Dog, you and your dog will be heeling along together. You will tell your dog to down, but you will keep moving with no hesitation. You may turn to face your dog as you tell him to down, and you can move away while facing him (so that you are walking backward). Still, you want this to be smooth and without any pauses. The second sign is (Turn) Call to Front, Finish R/L. So if you have not already turned to face your dog, you need to do so when you reach this sign. Call him to come and sit in front. Once he is sitting, tell him to finish; you can choose either the Finish to the Right or the Finish to the Left.

Halt, Stand for Exam—Return and Forward From Stand: You will have two signs for this bonus as well. The first is to Halt, Stand for Exam. You will heel up to the sign, and your dog will sit. Then tell him to stand. You may touch him to pose him, but you may not physically lift him up to a standing position. Once he is standing, make sure that you are in *heel* position and then tell or signal him to stand. You may do both. Now walk about 6 feet (2 m) away from your dog. Note: Do *not* back away. Once you are about 6 feet (2 m) away, turn and face your dog. The judge will come up and do a quick novice obedience exam—a touch on the head, shoulders, and rear. Once the judge is done, return to your dog by walking around him counterclockwise back into *heel* position and then move forward.

Halt, Leave Dog—Turn and Down: You will once again have two signs to complete this bonus. The first is a simple heel to a stop, halt, and have your dog sit in *heel* position. Then, tell him to stay and walk alone to the next sign, which will be about 10 feet (3 m) away. Turn to face your dog, and tell him to down. Ideally, he will not move forward at all but will drop down right in place. Once he is down—and that includes those elbows—you will return to him by walking counterclockwise around him to *heel* position. Once you are back, you are done! This exercise is a lead-in to Utility obedience signals.

Level 3

Turn, Halt, Retrieve, Finish: This sign packs a lot of effort into one exercise! If you are doing the bonus, give the ring steward an object for your dog to retrieve before you start your run. This could be a toy, a glove as is used in Utility, or an obedience dumbbell. While you are heeling with your dog to this sign, the steward or judge will place your retrieve object about 15 feet (4.5 m) away from the sign. (She will try to do this without attracting your dog's attention.) When you reach the sign, do an about turn. You are now facing the object that was placed behind your back. You will halt so that your dog is sitting by your side. Indicate the object to your dog, and tell him to retrieve or fetch it.

He must bring it back to you; ideally, he will sit in front while holding it. Take the item from him and then have him finish. You can choose which side to go to *heel* position.

During the Turn, Halt, Retrieve, Finish, your dog must retrieve an object.

Call Front, Back Up 3 Steps: For this bonus sign, start by heeling to the sign. Then back up, calling your dog to front. Once he is sitting, tell him to back up. He can stand first or he can start to back up while he is sitting. He must actually get up, however, and can't simply scoot backward while sitting. Your dog must back up three full steps while you are moving toward him. Ideally, he will stay straight in front of you. Once he has done the three steps, you are finished!

Halt, Leave Dog—Turn, Call Front (Distraction): This exercise starts off simply. Heel up to the sign and halt. Your dog will sit, and you will tell him to stay while you walk on to the next sign. At the second sign, turn and face your dog. The judge will be standing at your side but about 6 feet (2 m) away. As you call your dog to front, the judge will walk forward, passing your dog, who is coming to you. Once he has gone past the judge, the judge will turn and walk behind him. Ideally, your dog will totally ignore the judge, come straight to you, and sit in front. You do not need to do a Finish.

15

Rally Games

One of the best things about rally is that, once you are comfortable with the format, you can make up all kinds of fun games and activities that take advantage of basic training skills and mix in other dog sports—or you can simply have some silly fun. Dogs enjoy training with you no matter which version you decide to try!

Mixed Rally/Agility Course

If your dog also trains in agility, a mixed rally/agility course can be a lot of fun. At the beginner level, the course should be set so that everything can be done on lead, but for advanced dogs, you can certainly work off lead.

To do a mixed course of rally and agility, your dog will need some agility skills. To get started, I suggest *The Beginner's Guide to Agility,* by Laurie Leach. Design your course around the agility and rally skills your dog already has. For example, instead of using four cones for the weave-once Serpentine, stick in six weave poles. With careful lead handling, you can do this on lead, and your dog will get to practice some "real" weaves. Don't plan on weaving with him, however, because there won't be room!

An advanced dog who is comfortable working off lead could even do 12 weave poles, as long as you can find space on your course. Having a controlled rally exercise right before and after the weaves helps your dog learn to enter the weaves carefully and correctly and push through all the way at the end to move on to the next obstacle.

Jumps can also be worked in, just as in advanced rally classes. Keep the jump standards low, if possible, so that leashes don't get snagged as you run by. The jumps used for rally are similar to those used in obedience or agility—a panel or solid jump, a bar jump, and a broad jump.

This Corgi does some weaves on her course using weave poles instead of cones.

A 270-degree right turn could be followed by a teeter (seesaw). You will still need to number the course, and for some obstacles you may want a sign. In other cases, such as the teeter, it is fairly obvious what the dog needs to do.

Mixing rally and agility is a great help for the dog who needs work on "handler focus." Instead of heading off to do obstacles by himself, he must pay attention to you because there may be a sign like a 360-degree Left before he goes on to the A-frame. In both sports, you are allowed to use as much verbal encouragement as you need, and certainly hand signals and body language are important in both rally and agility.

When setting up a course that combines both rally and agility obstacles, think clearly about the path of both the person and the dog. You don't want someone tripping over a rally sign on her way around the course! If you want to include jumps, plan the spacing so that the dog has time to land safely and doesn't have to spin on a dime to make it back for the next exercise. If you are running multiple dogs, as in a class situation, set the spacing for the biggest dog. And don't forget to change jump heights between dogs if need be.

Tiny runs a chute tunnel as part of her fun rally course.

Reward both types of exercises equally so that your dog knows the treats are just as good for doing a rally exercise correctly as they are for hitting a contact or doing six weave poles flawlessly. By talking, encouraging, and verbally assisting your dog, you make both sports fun for him.

Mixing the two sports can also help a dog who tends to be independent in agility, running off at high speed on his own. He will quickly realize that it makes sense to stick near you and follow your guidance because it leads to good things, like treats or a game of tug. On the other hand, the dog who is a bit lackadaisical about rally may brighten up and get psyched when he figures out that tough rally exercises are mingled with fun, hard-running agility obstacles.

Rally Speak

In dog sports, we refer to handler focus and obstacle or work focus. There are times when our dogs need to look to us for guidance and direction. At other times, we want them to concentrate on the task at hand, such as clearing a jump.

Rally Caution

A course with just obedience doodling may not be fun for the average dog. Don't hesitate to mix in tricks, freestyle moves, or just silly games.

Obedience Exercises and Rally

Obedience exercises can also be mixed into a rally setting. In fact, some venues do that already, such as the APDT, with its retrieving and distance *recalls*. This is where your ingenuity at designing signs will come in handy. Check out the APDT Bonus signs and some of its unique Level 2 and Level 3 signs, which are often used in combinations.

Start by thinking of those obedience exercises you need to work on. Then take the exercise and break it down into tiny steps. For example, if your dog is having problems with the *recall*, you actually have at least five different steps to focus on: the *sit-stay*, the actual calling of the dog to come, sitting in front, finishing to the left, and finishing to the right.

Rally signs could include some of the following:

- Dog Sit, Stay, Walk 10 feet (3 m), Return
- Dog Sit, Stay, Handler Go 10 feet (3 m), Call and Release
- Dog Sit, Stay, Handler Go 10 feet (3 m), Call and Dog Sit in Front
- Dog Sit, Handler Go to Front Position, Dog Finish Left
- Dog Sit, Handler Go to Front Position, Dog Finish Right

By breaking the exercise down into tiny steps, you can see where your dog is having a problem and you can work on that problem without pattern training or getting him to anticipate it. Intersperse these signs with a variety of regular rally signs so that your dog still gets to do some interesting exercises.

Virtually every obedience exercise can be broken down into small steps that are perfect for rally. Having signs will help you to remember and work on the details that go into making a top-notch, precise obedience performance. Still, at least for much of your training, keep the rally motto in mind: It should be fun! Use the verbal and body language cues you need to help your dog. Once he is doing the exercise in the way you want, start cutting back on cues and randomizing their use. Keep up the positive rewards—praise, petting, treats, toys, and play. Your dog doesn't want to work for no payback.

Silly Games

One of the best uses for the rally format is to truly have fun making up silly games. Turn your imagination loose for some fun or funny exercises. Some examples include:

Put Hat on Dog, Remove Hat From Dog. For these two signs, you need a hat or bandana that can fit most dogs. Place the hat on a chair, and put a chair at the next station where the hat can be left. You'll also need a helper to return the hat to the first chair. A variation could have the handler wear the hat, or have both dog and handler wear hats!

Handler Sit, Sing Happy Birthday. Most dogs find signs like these to be truly funny. For this exercise, the handler and dog team heel up to a chair. The handler then sits in the chair and sings "Happy Birthday" to her dog. Some dogs may choose to sing along!

Mandy demonstrates a nice "shake."

Tricks

It can also be challenging to include tricks. Although not all of the participating dogs may know all of the tricks because handlers can lure, use hand signals, etc., most dogs can be guided into doing at least a reasonable facsimile of the tricks. For example, for the trick Bang, Bang, You're Dead, the use of a hand signal and a verbal for *down* will at least get most dogs on the ground.

Tricks that make for nice rally signs include Bang, Bang, You're Dead; Sit and Shake; Sit Up or Sit Pretty; Spin (Clockwise); Twirl (Counterclockwise); Roll Over; and Find Your Tail.

You may think that a rally course with tricks interspersed is just for kids, such as 4-H groups. I can tell you from experience, however, that adults enjoy these just as much and have a wonderful time, too.

If you are setting out a course for a breed specialty event, plan fun rally signs and games that revolve around that breed's heritage. This will be easier for some breeds than others. For example, for the herding breeds, signs involving fetching, penning, and gathering sheep toys would work very well. Retrievers can use duck toys for their retrieving and marking skills.

Herding-breed signs could include:

Fetch the Sheep. On the floor, place a sheep toy that your dog must bring to you. He then carries the toy to a particular spot as you heel by and leaves it there.

Pen the Sheep. Your dog must carry the toy and place it into a box on the floor.

Gather the Sheep. Three sheep toys are scattered on the floor, and your dog must collect all three and bring them to you.

For sporting dogs:

Fetch the Duck. On the floor, place a duck toy that your dog must bring to you. He then carries the toy to a particular spot as you heel by and leaves it there.

Mark the Duck. Place the duck toy out on the floor ahead of the station. Mark or point out the toy to your dog, who must visually focus on it. Then, either ask for a retrieve or ask the dog to walk by.

Terriers might enjoy games with soft, rat-like or squeaky toys such as:

Get the Rat. Place a soft toy inside a small children's tunnel. Your dog must go into the tunnel and fetch the toy.

Freestyle and Rally

Freestyle is a natural to combine with rally. There are an incredible number of freestyle moves, and virtually all those moves can be performed on both sides of the handler and sometimes in front or in back as well. Mixing in freestyle moves with rally gives your dog more variety, and it might induce you to try another sport. For freestyle, you are allowed to encourage your dog, and positive training and attitude are very important. Eventually, you will make your cues subtle or fade them almost entirely, but for beginner dogs, cues may need to be obvious.

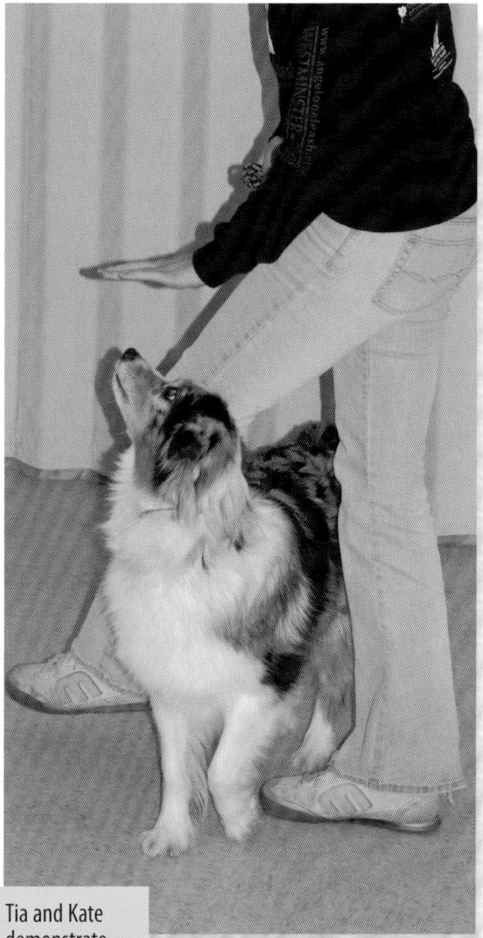

Tia and Kate demonstrate leg weaves.

Signs could include Weave Through Your Legs 3 Steps, Front to Back, Weave Through Your Legs, Back to Front, Spin on Left Side (counterclockwise), Spin in Front, Twirl on Right Side (clockwise), Twirl in Front, and Heel on the Right Side 5 Steps. These are all relatively simple freestyle moves. You can easily get more complicated or simulate some rally signs. The Back Up 3 Steps move could easily be part of a freestyle routine. The Left About Turn and the 360-degree moves could be included as well.

Good freestyle dogs are comfortable working all around their handlers.

Rally Profile

Mary, Mouse, and Miss JB

Mary Yates was attracted to rally back in 2001, when she was looking for fun things to do with her rescue Beagle, Miss JB. (That is JB for Just Beautiful.) Rally came up as a topic on the Beagle BOAT Internet list—Beagles in Obedience, Agility, and Tracking.

Right away, Mary found rally to be an excellent sport for dogs who either won't do obedience, such as her Beagle, or who can't do obedience, such as her wonderful Cardigan Welsh Corgi, Mouse, who was sidelined from obedience at the age of six by a disc rupture. "Despite immediate surgery and wonderful rehab, Mouse still couldn't handle the 10-inch-high (25.5-cm) jumps she needed to do for Utility obedience, but the 8-inch (20.5-cm) rally jumps were within her capabilities," reports Mary. Mouse went on to earn her RAE title from the AKC on April 1, 2007—no April Fool's Day for her!

Both of Mary's dogs enjoy the fact that rally involves speed, unpredictable courses, and a relaxed atmosphere. Doing *stays*, especially the Honor, has been a drag for them, but they handle it. Because Miss JB and Mouse had both done some obedience training, the Novice exercises were easy for them to learn. Doing the Call—Front from the sitting in *heel* position took more creativity and effort, as well as the Back 3 Steps. Mary now incorporates those moves into her training, including that with her new young Cardigan Welsh Corgi, Skunk.

Mary's only warning to someone trying to go back and forth between rally and obedience is to be careful about depending on extra verbal encouragement and extra hand signals.

Mixing rally and agility is a great help for the dog who needs work on handler focus.

They will side-pass on either side or while in front facing their handlers. These moves can be included in a rally-type course.

K-9 Dressage is a version of freestyle that is similar to rally in many ways. Dressage has a set course that is based around letter markers. You move from one marker to the next in the proper sequence while performing various tasks. It certainly sounds similar to rally, doesn't it? You won't get the hints that rally signs give you, however. You need to remember that you go from A to C, passing through B, but no sign will remind you that you do a Fast from A to B and then a Slow from B to C. The judge will announce the sequence, and you need to know what is involved. In between sequences, you can release your dog. Verbal praise and assistance are allowed throughout, and hand cues may also be used. Novice levels start on lead.

Resources

Most organizations have rules and regulations available for downloading on their websites, along with signs and training advice. Exercises are fairly similar across venues, so information from any site will still be valuable to you no matter what venue you choose to compete in. This applies to books and rally online groups as well.

Organizations

American Kennel Club
8051 Arco Corporate Drive, Suite 100
Raleigh, NC 27617-3390
Telephone: (919) 233-9767
Office Hours: Monday to Friday 8:30 a.m.–5:00 p.m. E.S.T.
Rally Regulations and Website
Telephone: (919) 816-3521
Fax: (919) 816-4204
E-Mail: rally@akc.org
www.akc.org/events/rally/

Association of Pet Dog Trainers (APDT)
APDT Rally Obedience
c/o Linda Sperco
31 Revere Avenue
Maplewood, NJ 07040
Telephone: 1-800-PET-DOGS
E-Mail: rallyo@apdt.com
Rally Regulations and website
www.apdt.com/po/rally/default.aspx

Australian Shepherd Club of America (ASCA)
www.asca.org
Rally Program Being Developed
pets.groups.yahoo.com/group/aussie-rally/

Canadian Association of Rally Obedience (CARO)
E-Mail: canadianrallyo@gmail.com
CARO, c/o Bev Hurst
6950 Cty Rd 10
VanKleek Hill, ON K0B 1R0
Rally Regulations and Website
www.canadianrallyo.ca/

Canadian Kennel Club (CKC)
The Canadian Kennel Club
200 Ronson Drive, Suite 400
Etobicoke, Ontario
M9W 5Z9
Office Hours: Monday to Friday 9:00 a.m.–5:00 p.m. E.S.T.
Telephone: (416) 674-3699
E-Mail: information@ckc.ca
Rally Regulations and Website
www.ckc.ca

United Kennel Club
100 E. Kilgore Road
Kalamazoo, MI 49002
Office Hours: Monday to Friday 9:00 a.m.–4:30 p.m. E.S.T.
Telephone: (269) 343-9020
Fax: (269) 343-7037
E-Mail: dvalva@ukcdogs.com
Rally Regulations and Website
www.ukcdogs.com

World Wide Kennel Club
P.O. Box 62
Mount Vernon, NY 10552
Telephone: (914) 771-5219
Fax: (914) 961-7789
E-Mail: wwkc1com@aol.com
Rally Regulations and Website
www.worldwidekennel.qpg.com

Books, Magazines, and Videos

Bergeman, Clarissa. *Ready to Rally!: A Video Guide to APDT Rally* DVD. In Canine Company, 2008.

Dearth, Janice. *The Rally Course Book: A Guide to AKC Rally Courses.* Crawford: Alpine Publications, 2004.

Dennison, Pamela. *Click Your Way to Rally Obedience.* Crawford: Alpine Publications, 2006.

Front and Finish Magazine. *P.O. Box 333. Galesburg, IL 61402-0333. Telephone:* 309-344-1333. http://frontandfinish.com.

Logue, Marie. *Rally Competition Record.* Lakeland: Prompt Typesetting Service, 2004.

Rally Sources for Books and Equipment

Country Dreams Webstore
Bud Houston's Country Dream Agility
14543 State Route 676
Waterford, OH 45786
Telephone: (740) 749-3597
www.dogagility.org/store rally books, rally magazines, and training guides

Dogwise a Direct Book Service Inc. Company
403 S. Mission St.,
Wenatchee WA 98801, USA
Telephone: (800) 776-2665
www.dogwise.com
rally books and signs

J & J Dog Supplies, Inc.
P.O. Box 1517
Galesburg, IL 61402
Telephone: (800) 642-2050
Fax: (309) 344-3522
www.jjdog.com
rally books, equipment, signs, and patches

K-9 Rally.com
Bea Moore
P.O. Box 20593
San Jose, CA, 95160
E-Mail: beamoore@comcast.net
www.k-9rally.com
rally books and signs

Max 200 Performance Dog Equipment, Inc.
2113 State Route 31
Port Byron, NY 13140
Telephone: (800) 446-2920
Fax: (315) 776-9603
www.max200.com
rally books, equipment, signs and patches

Rally Websites and E-Mail Groups

Check out the organizations and resources listed above as well. Some breeds will have their own groups under Yahoo groups, so check out groups such as

http://pets.groups.yahoo.com/group/aussie-rally
www.k-9rally.com
www.rallyobedience.com
http://pets.groups.yahoo.com/group/rally-obed

Other Websites

www.nylabone.com
www.tfh.com

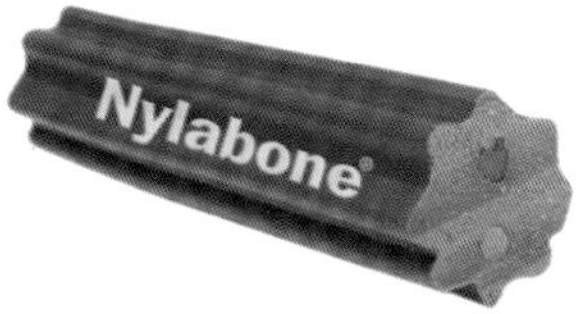

Index

Boldfaced numbers indicate illustrations.

A

B

C

D

E

F

G

H

I

J

K

L

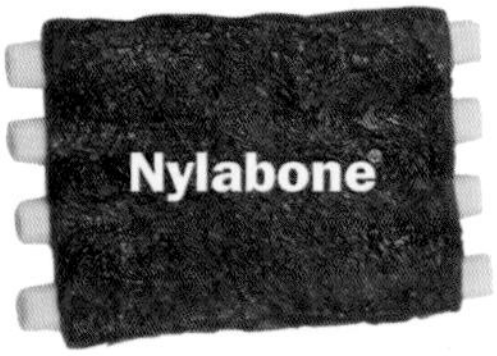

Q

R

S

T

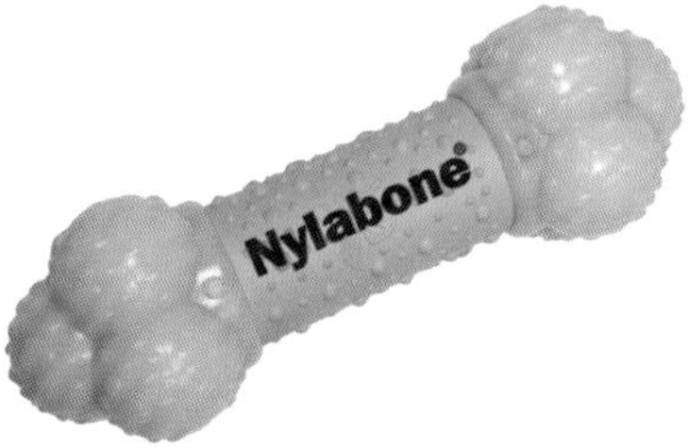
Nylabone®

Dedication

I would like to dedicate this book to the three wonderful dogs who earned their AKC rally titles at the amazing DOTCORNY trials over New Year's weekend in 2005. To Hokey, my wonderful Terv who was seven months old at the time and this was his first title. To Susan, the Corgi who came to me late in life—this was our last title together at age 13. To Dani, my wonderful Terv who has done everything for me and done it all well.

Acknowledgments

I would like to thank my agent, Jessica Faust of BookEnds—she never gives up! My editor at TFH, Stephanie Fornino, who has amazing patience and good humor. The various APDT members who had faith and helped a small 4-H club actually hold rally trials. Special thanks to those who shared their rally stories with me. Also, thank you to the AKC, which gave rally another dimension and which allowed us the use of its signs. As always, many thanks to the animals and humans who share my life, cover for me when I am caught up in working, make me laugh, and always, always, keep me humble.

About the Author

Debra M. Eldredge, DVM, is a veterinarian/writer and active participant in most dog sports. She graduated from Cornell University and was the first recipient of the Gentle Doctor Award. Dr. Eldredge is an award-winning writer with multiple Maxwells from the Dog Writers Association of America (DWAA) and Muse Medallions from the Cat Writers' Association, Inc. (CWA). She has competed in American Kennel Club (AKC) and Association of Pet Dog Trainers (APDT) rally with four dogs and earned multiple rally titles, including two RAEs. She currently has two Belgian Tervurens and also lives with another Belgian Tervuren, two Australian Shepherds, and a Pembroke Welsh Corgi who belong to her children—all rally titled. Dr. Eldredge lives on a small farm in upstate New York and also has cats, donkeys, a goat, sheep, ducks, and horses—none of whom do rally!

Photo Credits

0854601975 (Shutterstock): 69

Utekhina Anna (Shutterstock): 211

Peter Betts (Shutterstock): back cover

Tad Denson (Shutterstock): 136 (bottom)

Baevskiy Dmitry (Shutterstock): 123

Tom Eldredge: spine, 15, 16, 21, 38, 48, 51, 53, 56, 57, 58, 64, 73, 75, 93, 98, 104, 106, 113, 114, 118, 124, 130, 138, 141, 143, 144, 153, 155, 159, 188, 195, 206, 208, 209, 218, 219, 221, 223

Jean M. Fogle@jeanmfogle.com: 4, 80, 102, 116, 162, 172, 186

Eric Isselée (Shutterstock): 43, 154

Petr Jilek (Shutterstock): 46

kilukilu (Shutterstock): 77 (left)

Lois M. Kosch (Shutterstock): 215

Erik Lam (Shutterstock): 82, 95, 99, 147, 202

lightpoet: 1, 78

L.M.V (Shutterstock): 148, 149

Mrakoplas (Shutterstock): 216

Andrzej Mielcarek (Shutterstock): 39

Wendi Pencille: 22, 24, 26, 31, 34, 70, 87, 100, 126, 128, 136 (top), 164, 166, 177, 181, 197, 203

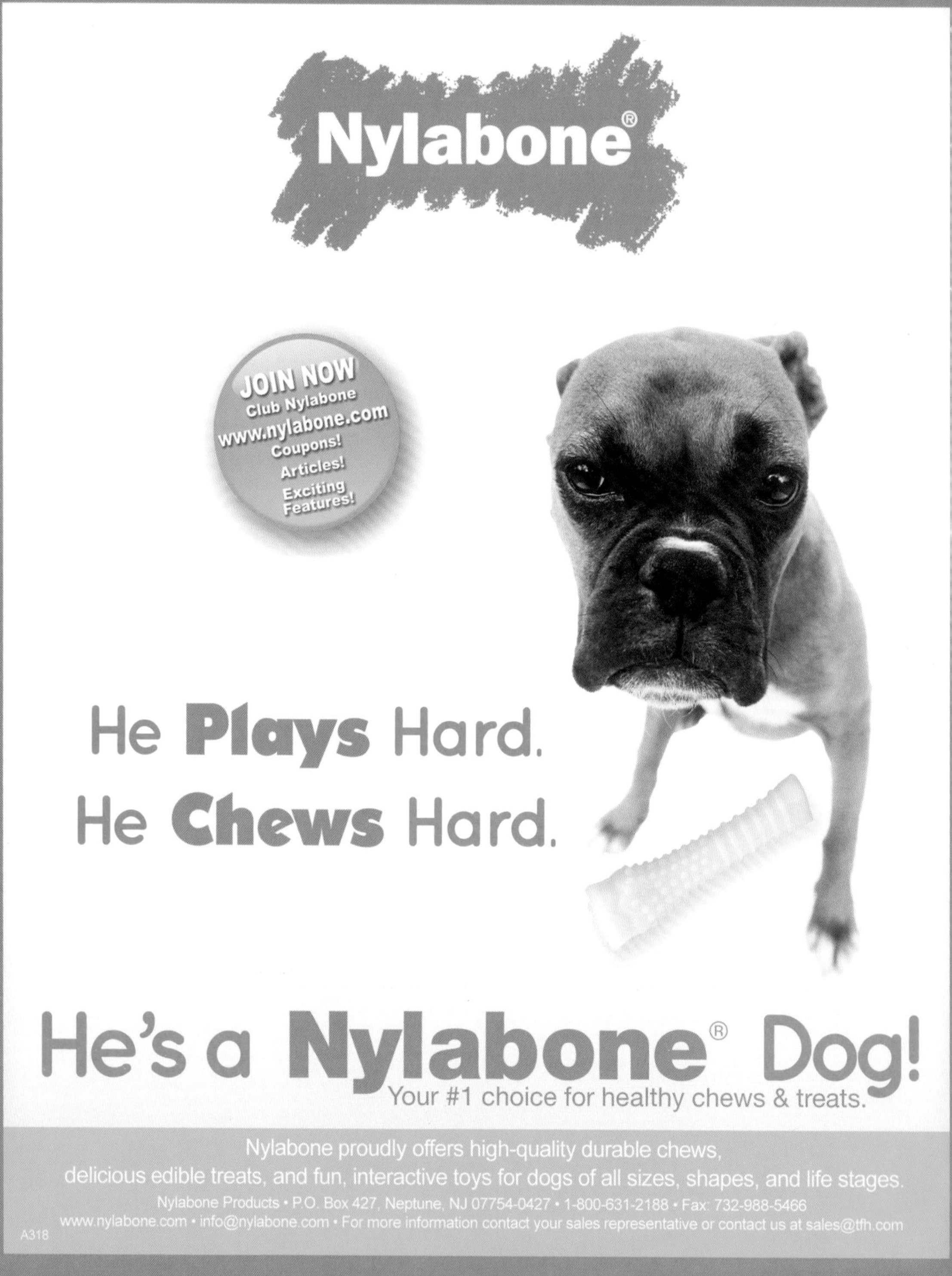
Nylabone®
JOIN NOW
Club Nylabone
www.nylabone.com
Coupons!
Articles!
Exciting Features!
He Plays Hard.
He Chews Hard.
He's a Nylabone® Dog!
Your #1 choice for healthy chews & treats.
Nylabone proudly offers high-quality durable chews,
delicious edible treats, and fun, interactive toys for dogs of all sizes, shapes, and life stages.
Nylabone Products • P.O. Box 427, Neptune, NJ 07754-0427 • 1-800-631-2188 • Fax: 732-988-5466
www.nylabone.com • info@nylabone.com • For more information contact your sales representative or contact us at sales@tfh.com
A318